God's Singers

Written by
Lisa Mayo Murphy
and
Leanne Mayo

Copyright © 2011
King's Peak Publications
All Rights Reserved

Fourth Printing

ISBN 13: 978-1456594152
ISBN 10: 145659415X
LCCN: 2011901812

King's Peak Publications
P.O. Box 910
Midway, Utah
84049
U.S.A.

Dedication

to

our dear family and friends…
with whom we feel inspired to share our love of the fine arts. This has been the impetus for us to create and share this book. Our hope is that a love for the lives and works of classic authors will extend to subsequent generations. Man's spiritual survival depends upon keeping alive the beauties of life in the hearts and minds of humankind forever.

Leanne Mayo

Lisa Mayo Murphy

Acknowledgments

To my mother, Leanne Mayo, who changed and enriched my life forever when she taught me to read as a preschooler, and who has shared my life's passion for all things literary. Like Elizabeth Barrett Browning, reading is not an option for me. It is essential to my well being. Without it, "the soul eats itself."

To my dearest brother, Michael, who had the soul of a poet.

Lisa Mayo Murphy

With gratitude to my husband, Raymond Mayo, whose constant assistance, counsel and encouragement have made this book possible.

To Lisa McClain-Mayo whose cheerfulness and competence were great assets in bringing our words to the page.

To Becky Paget whose artistic talents fitted my vision for the book perfectly.

To Mark Murphy for our beautiful cover design.

To Shaun Murphy whose technical expertise and belief in our project meant so much.

With appreciation to Karen and Walter Loewenstern who graciously shared their Rocky Mountain home in Beaver Creek, Colorado, where this book was begun, surrounded by the spectacle and splendor of nature's springtime.

Leanne Mayo

English Day on a Western Plain

Fog has quietly crept in,
A stranger from another land

Hangs in heavy stillness
On the brown, flat plain

Bearing tales of English hills,
Green grass, purple heather

To tumbleweed and thistle thorn
Quaffing cracked parchment

Only my breath moves this quietude,
A vapor of lingering curls

Whispering of bog fires and gentlewomen
Putting mittened hands to heavy paper

To pen the mists
Of hearts and minds,

Then vanishes into the white blanket
Softening sagebrush, spiny weed.

It's an English day on a Western plain.
Call me Charlotte or Emily or Jane.

~Lisa Mayo Murphy
Colorado, 1992

God's Singers

Contents

Prelude	i
Observations and Parallels	vii
Emily Dickinson "To Be Alive is Power"	1
Emily Brontë "No Coward Soul is Mine"	53
Christina Rossetti "Sing No Sad Songs for Me"	147
Elizabeth Barrett Browning "How Do I Love Thee?"	203
Postlude	273
Authors' Notes	274
Bibliography	278

Prelude
By Lisa Mayo Murphy

There have been times when I've been reading poetry and I wonder if what I'm reading should be called scripture. Other than sacred writings, nothing comes closer to truth or is as worthwhile to read than poetry. It speaks to the soul and draws one back again and again, becoming more meaningful and beautiful with every reading. Anatole Broyard said:

> *"Unless we read poetry, we'll never have our hearts broken by language... or healed."*

In the Japanese language, the word for poet translates into English as, "a person who sings." Elizabeth Barrett Browning didn't know this, but it was she who called a poet, *"one of God's singers."* She opined:

> *"A poet is a human creature too weak to bear his human pain."*

She would know; she was one of them, as am I.

Good poetry ages and ripens well. It speaks truth. It never grows old. Rather, it grows on you and with you. Like scripture, it is timeless and true for every generation. Emily Dickinson declared that we need poetry to help us understand life's complexities.

Women writers are relatively new to the literary world. Until 200 years ago, they were not considered intelligent enough to write and publish. In a male dominated world, women writers tried to hide their female identity by writing unsigned or using pseudonyms. Many used male pen names. Mary Ann Evans wrote as George Eliot. Amandine Lucille Aurora Dupin wrote as George Sand. The Brontë sisters first published as Currer, Ellis and Acton Bell. Female authors still use initials to hide their gender. Consider Harry Potter author, J.K. Rowling.

In addition to the old adage: "Children should be seen, but not heard," there could have been another one: "Women should be seen, but not read."

A perfect example of the lack of acceptance of women as writers is an incident that occurred on July 8, 1889, when Robert Browning—only six months before his death—glanced into a newly published volume of Edward Fitzgerald's letters, collected after Fitzgerald's death. The letter was dated July 15, 1861:

> *"Mrs. Browning's Death is a relief to me, I must say… A woman of real Genius, I know; but what is the upshot of it all? She and her sex had better mind the kitchen and their children and perhaps the Poor; except in such things as little Novels, they only devote themselves to what Men do much better…"*

When Robert found this letter, Elizabeth had been dead for thirty-eight years! But he was still, as Elizabeth had said, *"a master in clenched passion."* Though Fitzgerald was dead, Robert wrote a rebuttal to his letter in the form of a poem:

> *"I chanced upon a new book yesterday:*
> *I opened it, and where my finger lay*
> *'Twixt page and uncut page these words I read*
> *--Some six or seven at most – and learned thereby*
> *That you, FitzGerald, whom by ear and eye*

She never knew, 'thanked God my wife was dead.'

Ay, dead! and were yourself alive, good Fitz,
How to return you thanks would task my wits:
Kicking you seems the common lot of curs –
While more appropriate greeting lends you grace:
Surely to spit there glorifies your face –
Spitting – from lips once sanctified by Hers.

The entire nineteenth century produced only four women poets whose significance has endured to the present day:

- *Emily Dickinson*
- *Emily Brontë*
- *Christina Rossetti*
- *Elizabeth Barrett Browning*

I discovered the writings of these four women when I was in my late twenties. Perhaps I had read their poetry in a high school literature class. If I did, I don't remember. I did not have the breadth of life experience to grasp what I was reading at that time. But in my twenties, after I had been waylaid by life a few times, the words of Christina Rossetti brought me to tears at the first reading.

I discovered her when I first heard what I thought to be the most beautiful Christmas song I'd ever heard, "In The Bleak Midwinter," on a holiday recording by the King's College Choir of Cambridge. I had never heard the song before; but the tune was so haunting and the words so beautiful, I found myself pushing the replay button over and over again and copying the words onto paper as I heard them. When I had finished transcribing the song, I looked at the words and thought to myself, 'This isn't just a song. This is someone's poem that has been set to music.'

Now I was on the hunt. These were the days before internet. My next step to solve the mystery of these words that affected me so deeply was to go to the library. I pulled a book of poetry off the shelf and turned to the Index of First Lines, and there it was. Aha! I was right! This *was* a work of poetry — by someone I'd never heard of — a woman named Christina Rossetti. 'Who was this person?' I wondered, 'And what else did she write?'

So began my beautiful journey into the world of poetry — a world that would soon become an essential part of me. I was so affected by Christina's poems that I copied them and pasted them into my own journals. I read them over and over again. I found such comfort in her words that I felt as though she had been sent to me by some divine loving power who knew my need for solace.

The more I read, the more I wanted to know, 'Who was this person who could write such words that they sink into the depths of my soul like a prayer?'

At this point my mother added her fire to this search, and we began sleuthing together. Our task was to discover the identity and character of Christina Rossetti. As we researched the details of her life and put her poetry into the context of her life experience, we found that we not only loved Christina's poetry, but we loved Christina as well. We felt as though we had found a long lost soul sister who had left us a trail of words by which we could find her from another century and merge our souls across time.

And so we began our journey to find our other lost poetic sisters. But now, we knew where to look, for they each left the deepest parts of themselves on paper — words and poems that would call to their kindred throughout the ages.

We found three more women with whose poetry and life stories we also fell in love. Two are called Emily, the other is named Elizabeth. These four are the first women who dared to write the interior of their hearts and minds. They are, indeed, worthy to be called *God's Singers*.

Our literary journey was not yet over. Joy is meant to be shared, and we felt that our findings were too good to keep to ourselves. We began to share our new-found passion with friends who were similarly moved by what they learned. Like us, they found the poetry on its own to be sublime. But when coupled with the life stories of its authors, the experience and appreciation of it was deepened immeasurably.

Before long, we were traveling to book groups and schools to share our findings with a wider audience. The next logical step was to create this book, so that you, too, can have ready access to these poetic treasures of truth and the women who created them.

We found that we could not write about our poets without writing about their families as well. Here you will find four fascinating family stories as well as four poet biographies. As I read and wrote about our poets, I sometimes related so closely to them that I felt as though I was inside their heads. I understood their feelings and motivations. I was moved and inspired, again and again, by their passion for life, beauty, expression and their dedication to their art. Ellen Moers, in her book <u>Literary Women</u>, writes that reading the poetry of Christina Rossetti, Emily Brontë, Elizabeth Barrett Browning and Emily Dickinson together is like *"uncorking a bottle of rare wine."*

It is our hope that you, dear reader, are similarly touched with as much joy, solace and enrichment as we have been, as you discover the fascinating women behind some of the finest poetry ever written.

Observations and Parallels

Five days after Christina Rossetti's birth on December 5, 1830, Emily Dickinson was born in Amherst, Massachusetts on the other side of the Atlantic. Elizabeth Barrett was twenty-four, already a published poet, and living as a recluse in a nearby London neighborhood. Emily Brontë, age twelve, was immersed in her imaginary world of Gondal on the Yorkshire Moors.

Although they never met, they were greatly influenced by each other. They read each other's work, which encouraged them in their new female poetic art at a time when most others were questioning whether women should be writing poetry at all. Emily Dickinson avowed that she refused to be *"shut up in prose"* and kept a picture of Elizabeth Barrett Browning on her bedroom wall. She was moved to write the following poetic tribute to Charlotte Brontë at her death:

Charlotte Brontë's Grave

All overgrown by cunning moss,
　All interspersed with weed,
The little cage of 'Currer Bell.'
　In quiet Haworth laid.

The bird, observing others,
　When frosts too sharp became,
Retire to other latitudes,
　Quietly did the same,

But differed in returning:
  Since Yorkshire hills are green,
Yet not in all the nests I meet
  Can nightingale be seen.

Gathered from many wanderings,
  Gethsemane can tell
Through what transporting anguish
  She reached the asphodel!

Soft fall the sounds of Eden
  Upon her puzzled ear:
Oh, what an afternoon for heaven,
  When 'Brontë' entered there!

It was a time of momentous literary flowering in the English language. The United States and England were littered with literary greats. They published on both continents. Many of them crossed the oceans to meet each other.

In Victorian England, a few literary contemporaries of the Brontë's, Browning's, and Rossetti's were Wordsworth, Dickens, Coleridge, Carlyle, Austen, Tennyson and Thackeray. They were members of

London's high society and many of them vacationed together in the Lake District.

Emily Dickinson's New England found Emerson, Thoreau, Alcott and Hawthorne living and working side by side in Concord, Massachusetts. Longfellow lived down the road in Cambridge. In neighboring Connecticut, Harriet Beecher Stowe and Mark Twain were neighbors for a time.

In researching the lives of these four major poets, we made several distinct observations. We compiled a list of thirteen parallels of our poets' lives that absolutely astounded us. To find so many parallels is truly remarkable. To have lived with so many similarities in their lives, one can't help but conjecture about the psychology that these parallels had on our poets.

The Thirteen Parallels

1. They were all from very close-knit families, and, in several cases, large families.
    a. The children were born in quick succession. In the Brontë and Browning families, the mothers died leaving small children.
    b. Their fathers did not want them to marry. Thus, there are very few descendants from the four family lines.
    c. Including all three Brontë sisters, Charlotte, Emily and Anne, we have six poets for our parallels. Of these six women, only two ever married: Charlotte Brontë married only nine months before her death; Elizabeth Barrett

Browning was married for 15 years before her death.
2. Writing was in their genes! Their parents and siblings were also poets, writers and artists. All of our poets were frustrated when their brothers entered a world of education and opportunity that they were denied because they were girls.
3. They began writing when they were very young. The Brontë's and the Rossetti's wrote as very small children. Elizabeth Barrett and Christina Rossetti published in their teens. All of them were in full bloom as poets in their early thirties.
4. They were visionary, metaphysical poets. Their writings were religious in tone, using Biblical imagery and symbolism.
5. They all wrote about nature with great love and inspiration.
6. They wrote of unrequited love. They had infatuations with married men. They lived lives of longing, daydreaming and yearning from afar. Emily Dickinson said that all the men she loved were married.
7. They were prolific letter writers. Writing letters replaced personal relationships in their lives and sometimes diminished their creative energies.
8. All of them were passionately expressive. (Longfellow wrote, *"What is a poet without expression? A pipe without fire."*) Yet, paradoxically, they lived lives of seclusion and closely guarded privacy.
9. They were all reclusive. Emily Dickinson would not even let her doctor see her in person. He had to communicate with her through a closed door.

10. They were tiny women with short, slender, plain features. Emily Brontë was the tallest; yet still she was small. Four of the six (all three Brontë sisters and Emily Dickinson) had chestnut red hair.
11. All suffered with health problems throughout their lives. Emily Brontë and Elizabeth Barrett Browning suffered from anorexia. Illness was one of the few tools that Victorian women had to control their lives in a male dominated world.
12. They all had death fixations. They wrote about death and resignation.
13. Each of them was considered peculiar by the cultural norms of the day.

Comparison Chart

Event	Emily Dickinson	Christina Rossetti	Emily Brontë	Elizabeth Barrett Browning
Birth Date	10 December 1830	5 December 1830	30 July 1818	6 March 1806
Birth Place	Amherst, Mass.	London, England	Thornton, England	Coxhoe Hall, Durham, England
Number of Siblings	2	3	5	11
Father's Work	Lawyer	Professor	Curate	Businessman
Marriage	None	None	None	Yes, 15 years Robert Browning
Date of Death	May 15, 1886	Dec. 29, 1894	Dec. 19, 1848	June 29, 1861
Age at Death	55	64	30	55
Burial Place	Amherst, Mass.	Highgate Cemetery, London, England	Haworth, Yorkshire, England	Protestant Cemetery, Florence, Italy
First Published	10 poems while alive; first published posthumously in 1890	Age 17 Grandfather printed poems 1847	Religious poems, 1846; _Wuthering Heights_, 1847	Age 13 Father printed epic poem 1819

Emily Elizabeth Dickinson
1830 – 1886

Emily Dickinson took both her first and last breaths in the same house in Amherst, Massachusetts. The Homestead was built by her grandfather, Samuel Fowler Dickinson, in 1813, to house the Massachusetts monarch and his family. Perched on a grassy knoll near the university he founded, it sat like a sentinel on a hill with a pillared porch, numerous chimneys, high ceilings, double parlors, expansive hallways and bedrooms the size of sitting rooms. It was a symbol of the wealth and weight of the Dickinson name.

By the time Emily was born on December 10, 1830, the Dickinson's were already a distinguished old family in a new country. They were among the first European settlers to come from England in 1630 with John Winthrop, and they fought in the Revolutionary War.

Emily's grandfather, a lawyer, founded Amherst College. Her father, Edward Dickinson, the oldest of nine children, followed in his father's footsteps and also practiced law, was a judge and was treasurer of Amherst College for thirty-seven years. He carried on the family tradition of political activism and served in both the state and federal legislatures. The Homestead was the center of Amherst society, often hosting political and social events, including the annual Amherst College commencement receptions.

In 1826, Edward Dickinson, age twenty-three, was attracted to a young woman from the neighboring village of Monson, Massachusetts. He knew what he wanted in a future wife and chose carefully. He wrote, *"I have long…felt much interest in having [women] correctly instructed, & their tastes and judgments properly formed."* He judged Emily Norcross, aged twenty-two, to be a young woman *"in whom so many of the female virtues are conspicuous."* She was quiet, modest, dutiful and obedient. After two years of courtship he dispassionately proposed, promising her *"a life of rational happiness"* and presented his terms:

> *"My life must be a life of business, of labor and application to the study of my profession."*

When he asked Joel Norcross for his daughter's hand in marriage, he explained that he was *"partial"* to Emily and that he hoped to become *"her legal guardian & protector."* With his authority firmly established, the cool tone of formality in the Dickinson home was fixed.

Emily gave birth to three children in the next four years — a son and two daughters. She gave her own name, Emily, to her first daughter.

- (1829-1895) Austin William
- (1830-1886) Emily Elizabeth
- (1833-1899) Lavinia (Vinnie)

Lavinia later wrote that she grew up in a home of *"systematic privacy."* It was orderly, reserved and largely void of intimacy and affection. Her father was often away on business — but when he was home, he presided over his household with kingly expectations. Her mother was prone to depression and never expressed herself directly to anyone. She was quiet and distant while meticulously fulfilling the responsibilities of a proper housewife, never leaving a physical need of her family unmet. Despite their mother's attentiveness to their physical care, her emotional remoteness led Emily, the poet, to later recollect, *"I never really had a mother."*

Possessed of a high degree of intellect and sensitivity, young Emily came to view her mother as rather mechanical, saying, *"Mother doesn't care for thought."* Years later, after her mother's severe bouts of depression, she ruminated:

> *"How do people live without any thoughts? How do they get the strength to put on their clothes in the morning?"*

As their mother gradually withdrew, the Dickinson children became increasingly dependent upon each other for emotional support and stability. This sibling relationship would carry them throughout their lives, compensating for the lack of parental attention and love. At the same time, the motherless Brontë children were likewise rearing themselves on the Yorkshire moors in England.

In later years, Lavinia described her family culture as one of solid boundaries:

> *"While contributing to the maintenance of a solid front, each component part remained distinct and independent... (We) all lived like friendly and absolute monarchs, each in his own domain. You were bound to those to whom you gave loyalty and devotion, but with whom you did not share your thoughts."*

It is not hard to see how Emily's independent spirit was fostered, having come from such a family tradition of privacy and isolation. Her chosen seclusion in later life would not have been such a long leap from her early childhood training.

Even though the inhabitants of The Homestead were isolated from each other, their family was highly connected in Amherst society and young Emily was fully engaged in it. She enjoyed going to parties and playing games. She had girlhood crushes on boys with its accompanying girlish gossip and giggles. Of going on sleigh rides and country excursions, she wrote to an uncle, *"Amherst is alive with fun this winter..."*

In her mother's kitchen, she learned the one domestic art that would bring her lifelong pleasure — baking. In 1856, she even entered her bread at an Agricultural Fair and took second place. The following year, she served on the committee, judging the rye and Indian bread categories.

Emily's family culture may have been short on emotion, but it was long on intellect. The Dickinson family philosophy was built upon a foundation of education.

The Homestead was full of books — both classic and contemporary. Emily read voraciously even though she received mixed messages from her father about female education. She wrote, *"Father buys me many Books — but begs me not to read them — because he fears they joggle the Mind."* Her copies of Shakespeare, the Bible and Webster's Dictionary were well worn. She admired the work of Charlotte and Emily Brontë. But the female poet she idolized most was Elizabeth Barrett Browning — whose picture she hung on her bedroom wall.

The Dickinson's kept current on local and world news with their many subscriptions to newspapers and periodicals. They also hosted a steady stream of notables of the day at The Homestead because of Edward's involvement in the political and academic communities.

When the time came for Emily to acquire her secondary education at age sixteen, she could not go to the school that her grandfather had founded. Amherst College was for men only. Instead, her father sent her to Mount Holyoke Female Seminary in nearby South Hadley in 1847. She stood out as an original thinker from the start. She impressed and confounded her teachers. Her brother, Austin, remembered:

> "...her compositions were unlike anything ever heard — and always produced a sensation — both with the scholars and Teachers — her imagination sparkled — and she gave it free rein."

At Mount Holyoke one of the most formative experiences of her life took place. Amherst was afire with the religious fervor that earned the region the sobriquet, *"the burned over district."* The New England countryside was rife with revivals and the citizenry of Amherst was *"flocking to the ark of safety,"* as Emily put it. Mary Lyon, Mount Holyoke's evangelistic founder, held plenary assemblies for the girls three times a week in which they were put under immense pressure to confess Jesus as their Savior. The students were classified into three groups — Christians, Hopers and No-Hopers.

Emily resisted pressure from every direction, not only from adult authorities, but also from her many friends who were confessing Christ. Even her father, the imperious Edward Dickinson, had converted. It may have appeared that she was simply being stubborn and digging in her heels. The truth of the matter was that she was giving the question of God more thought than anyone else. She wrote to some of her more pious friends:

> *"I am one of the lingering bad ones, and so do I slink away, and pause, and ponder, and ponder, and pause..."*

These lines render a startling portrait of a young woman possessed of such unusual strength and honesty that she chose to maintain her personal integrity rather than to succumb to peer pressure or her own adolescent need to belong. She wrote of her lonely wrestle with religion to another friend:

> *"How lonely this world is growing, something so desolate creeps over the spirit and we don't know its name, and it won't go away, either Heaven is seeming greater, or Earth a great deal more small...Christ is calling everyone here, all my companions have answered, even my darling Vinnie believes she loves,*

*and trusts him, and I am standing alone in rebellion,...they all believe they have found; I can't tell you **what** they have found, but **they** think it is something precious. I wonder if it **is**?"*

Emily's reluctance to convert was grounded in truth and sincerity. She was astute enough to recognize mass hysteria when she saw it, and she was afraid of being deceived. After years of ruminating on the difference between truth and deception and the difficulty of discerning between the two, she captured on paper her experience with the perpetual quandary of what is human and what is divine:

> *Much Madness is divinest Sense--*
> *To a discerning Eye--*
> *Much Sense--the starkest Madness--*
> *'Tis the Majority*
> *In this, as All, prevail--*
> *Assent--and you are sane--*
> *Demur--you're straightway dangerous--*
> *And handled with a Chain--*

She wrote her friend, Abiah Root, with characteristic candidness:

> *"I was almost persuaded to be a Christian. I thought I never again could be thoughtless and worldly. But I soon forgot my morning prayer or else it was irksome to me. One by one my old habits returned, and I cared less for religion than ever."*

She ultimately embraced the label No-Hoper with the cynical humor that would show through much of her writing. When her lifelong friend, Helen Hunt Jackson, injured her foot, Emily wrote to her:

> *"Knew I how to pray, to intercede for your (broken) Foot were intuitive but I am but a No-Hoper."*

Emily knew that she believed in God. She simply was not sure of the nature of God. The established definition of God that was spoon-fed to her in her early years, and then shoved down her throat in her teens, simply did not ring true with her. If she had given in to peer and authoritarian pressure, she would have been untrue to herself; thereby, untrue to God, as she could know Him. Unlike Christina Rossetti, who sacrificed all for Jesus Christ, Emily found heaven to be an insufficient barter for autonomy. Consequently, with an unusually high degree of self-possession for a girl who was not yet twenty, Emily Dickinson took the lonely *"path less traveled by,"* as Robert Frost would call it a century later.

Upon leaving Mount Holyoke as one of the few No-Hopers, she wrote again to Abiah Root affirming the choice she had made:

> *"You are growing wiser than I am, and nipping in the bud fancies which I let blossom — perchance to bear no fruit, or if plucked, I may find it bitter. The shore is safer, Abiah, but I love to buffet the sea — I can count the bitter wrecks here in these pleasant waters, and hear the murmuring winds, but oh, I love the danger!"*

She had refused the faith but not with indifference. She often identified herself with Jacob, of the Old Testament, who wrestled with the Lord and asked for a blessing. She had, indeed, commenced her own wrestle with the

Lord, and it would inform her poetry for the rest of her life.

She returned to The Homestead where she became the quintessential homebody. From this time forward, she would live a life of her own choosing — choosing her own environment, choosing her friends, choosing her own work and words, choosing her personal form of faith - all very carefully. She would later say, *"The Soul Selects her own Society."* For the duration of her life, some forty years, she would leave The Homestead only four times, reluctantly, to embark on unwanted trips.

Now on the cusp of womanhood and living at home, Emily was expected to span an impossible divide. It was as if, until now, she had traveled across a great plain on a path well marked with all the books, political discussion and intellectual stimulation that she could want, for her father had treated her no differently than her brother when it came to her education. However, upon reaching her eighteenth year, she was stopped abruptly in her track, just as was Elizabeth Barrett when she reached of age.

Emily was now a young woman in a world that expected her to use her time and talents to comfort a husband and tend home and children. But her brilliant mind had already been fired, and she had developed a sharpened sense of independence when she followed her conscience at Holyoke. She was unable to unquestioningly switch gears. There was no seamless transition between her intellectually unrestrained childhood and the established path of restrained Victorian womanhood. She teetered on the edge of a canyon of doubt between the two worlds. Leaping the divide was impossible for her. She found that she favored the lonely wanderings in the dark narrows of the canyon below, *"The Brain has Corridors – surpassing,"* to the stifling, crowded plain above:

> *Behind Me -- dips Eternity --*
> *Before Me -- Immortality --*
> *Myself -- the Term between --*

Her avoidance of the sphere of women may have been one of self-preservation. All around her, women were disappearing. She was deeply affected by the loss of five girlhood friends to tuberculosis in one year. Her surviving friends also effectively disappeared into their husbands' lives when they married. Her view of marriage is unmistakable in the following poem:

> *"I'm wife"*
> *I've finished that –*
> *I'm "woman" now –*
> *It's safer so –*

Referencing the separation she felt from the world of women, she wrote with flippant humor to her friend, Jane, in 1850:

> *"The Sewing Society has commenced again, and held its first meeting last week – now all the poor will be helped – the cold warmed – the warm cooled – the hungry fed – the thirsty attended to – the ragged clothed – and this suffering – tumbled down world will be helped to it's feet again – which will be quite pleasant to all. I dont attend – notwithstanding my high approbation – which must puzzle the public exceedingly. I am already set down as one of those brands almost consumed – and my hardheartedness gets me many prayers."*

Being fully aware of her intellectual capabilities, yet unable to pursue them in the world beyond her home, she vented her frustration in a letter to her longtime friend and future sister-in-law, Susan Gilbert, who was then teaching in Baltimore. Her father delivered the letter to Susan when he attended a Whig convention there in 1852. She wrote:

> *"Why can't I be a Delegate to the great Whig convention? — dont I know all about Daniel Webster, and the Tariff, and the Law?-- ...I don't like this country at all..."*

However, she was dealt an even deeper wound that hit much closer to home as her intellect and writing were dismissed, even scorned by her own father. Now that the Dickinson children were grown, her brother, Austin, was lionized as the heir apparent to the Dickinson legacy. Anything that Emily had to offer was considered insignificant in comparison, just as the Brontë sisters' talents were shelved by their father whose hopes and dreams all rested in his less talented only son.

While Emily's brother went away to pursue higher education, his father prepared a place for him in his law firm and at Amherst College. He eagerly awaited Austin's letters as though each was a precious jewel. After reading them to himself, he would read them aloud to the family, remarking on their depth and eloquence, even comparing them to Shakespeare and promising to have them published for the family library. The letters would then be read again and again to anyone who came to the house.

Emily knew that writing was the ultimate battleground of competition with Austin—one in which she could prevail as well as accomplish the ultimate rebellion against her father. Perhaps this was the match that first lit Emily's fire for writing.

Although the men in her household disregarded her work, Emily's greatest benefactor was her sister, Lavinia, who she affectionately called Vinnie. Thinking and writing is solitary work. It takes a tremendous amount of time. In order to pursue their creative genius, artists must have patrons and benefactors. Vinnie, who also never married, unknowingly fulfilled the role of Emily's benefactor when she took over the daily maintenance of the household as their mother's physical and mental health declined. This freed up Emily to think and write, declaring, *"I prefer pestilence to housework."* Many years later, Vinnie would reflect:

> *"…as for Emily, she was not withdrawn or exclusive, really, she had to **think**, she was the only one of us that had that to do."*

In making her writing a priority, Emily began to limit herself to a few carefully chosen friends who stimulated her mind and her writing. Most of them were well known intellectuals of their day. She maintained these relationships primarily by letter writing. She mused that a letter is *"… a mind without corporeal friend."*

Through her copious correspondences she began her experimentation with words and phrases. It is from these extant letters that we have learned the few details we know of her life and the workings of her mind. We can also see the metamorphosis of her writing:

> *This is my letter to the world,*
> *That never wrote to me,--*
> *The simple news that Nature told,*
> *With tender majesty.*
> *Her message is committed*
> *To hands I cannot see;*
> *For love of her, sweet countrymen,*
> *Judge tenderly of me!*

Emily's most intimate and lifelong friend was Sue Gilbert. Though they came from entirely different backgrounds, the two women became passionately intense friends when they were in their early twenties. While Emily came from privilege and distinction, Sue was orphaned by the time she was eleven years old. After her alcoholic father left her in debt and in disgrace, she was shunted to a married sister whose husband resented being saddled with his wife's dependent younger sister. Sue was smart, strong and determined to remake herself into an independent, respectable woman as she patched her dresses and worried about having a roof over her head.

The entire Dickinson family was enamored with Sue. She appealed to their New England sense of determination and hard work. Emily was particularly attracted to Sue's spiritual depth and intellect. The emotion that sealed their bond was a shared sense of motherlessness — though Sue's mother was absent, Emily's mother was remote. They found in each other a measure of a mother's *"love, and influence, and ...sympathy"* that they missed. Sue was also a thinker and a writer. She was one of the few people who could meet Emily's intensity of thought. To Emily, Sue was a rare, treasured jewel.

By the spring of 1853, Austin, then a student at Harvard, was courting his younger sister's best friend with strong encouragement from Emily. With her heart set on Sue becoming a member of the Dickinson family, Emily courted Sue as assiduously as Austin did. Her letters to the object of their mutual affection were even more ardent than his. When her best friend and brother married, Emily was overjoyed. Now their sisterhood was legal.

The young couple moved into The Evergreens, an estate that Father Dickinson had built for them next door to The Homestead. Emily's dearest friend and confidant would never be far from her. Indeed, the two women wore a narrow path between their two houses that Emily described as *"just wide enough for two who love."* When they were not marking the path, letters swiftly flew between the two women whose houses stood side by side. In fact, Emily sent Sue more letters and poems over the years than to any other correspondent. Among the hundreds of poems and letters that Emily sent to Sue over the years, was a poetic tribute to the sister of her heart:

Emily Dickinson

*One Sister have I in our house,
And one, a hedge away.
There's only one recorded,
But both belong to me.*

*One came the road that I came --
And wore my last year's gown --
The other, as a bird her nest,
Builded our hearts among.*

*I spilt the dew --
But took the morn --
I chose this single star
From out the wide night's numbers --
Sue - forevermore!*

The other female constant in Emily's life was her childhood friend, Helen Hunt Jackson, a progressive writer and champion of Native Americans. She regularly encouraged Emily to publish her poetry over the years, to no avail, again referring to a poet as a singer:

> *"You are a great poet – and it is a wrong to the day you live in, that you will not sing aloud. When you are what men call dead, you will be sorry you were so stingy."*

The rest of Emily's circle of friends were men. Samuel Bowles and Josiah Holland were the editor and assistant editor, respectively, of "The Springfield Republican." She first came into contact with them when she anonymously published her first poem in their newspaper at age twenty-two:

> *"Awake ye muses nine, sing me a strain divine,*
> *Unwind the solemn twine, and tie my Valentine!"*

She became friends with both Sam and Josiah and their wives, Mary and Elizabeth. Sam printed several of Emily's poems in his newspaper over the years, including "The Snake," which was submitted by Sue, without Emily's consent.

Sam was a frequent visitor at Sue and Austin's home, The Evergreens. He was not as indulgent of Emily's penchant for privacy as others were, calling her the *"Queen of Recluse"* in a note written to Austin in 1863. An anecdotal story is told that when Bowles paid Emily a visit in 1877, she refused to come down the stairs to see him. He shouted up to her:

> *"Emily, you damn rascal. No more of this nonsense. I've traveled all the way from Springfield to see you. Come down at once."*

The tale continues that when she finally came down, she was never more engaging, as if she had never been coerced into showing herself.

It has been conjectured by some, but never proven, that Emily was secretly in love with Sam Bowles, even though he was married and unattainable.

Another correspondent and confidant in the poet recluse's small circle, who it has been speculated that Emily may have had a crush on, was a charismatic clergyman named Reverend Charles Wadsworth. She first heard him preach in

Washington D.C. when she was twenty-five years old during one of her few trips away from home. Sensing a kindred spirit of solitude and romance in Wadsworth, Emily initiated a lifelong correspondence with him, even calling him, *"my dearest earthly friend."* Their letters consisted largely of spiritual matters, which was Emily's great interest. She welcomed the challenge of Wadsworth's Calvinistic orthodoxy after having been greatly influenced by the transcendentalism of Ralph Waldo Emerson and Emily Brontë. She enjoyed the stretching of her mind between the two polarities of thought as she sought to articulate her own understanding of God.

By the time Emily entered her late twenties, her writing had become a great adventure of the mind. When she wrote, she felt her mind come alive. It was as though the words themselves were infused with a life force. Many times, she referred to words and poems as living things:

> *"A word is dead when it is said, some say. I say it just begins to live that day."*

The words fed her and she, in turn, fed them, creating an independent, self-sustaining cycle of life giving words, words giving life.

Emily's literary advisor was Thomas Wentworth Higginson, a champion of abolition and women's rights who surmised:

> *"The real disadvantage of women has lain in being systematically taught from childhood*

that it is their highest duty to efface themselves, or at least keep out of sight."

She first came into contact with him when she responded to his invitation, as the literary editor of "The Atlantic Monthly," for unknown poets to send in their work to his magazine. She sent him four poems, asking him if he were *"too deeply occupied to say if my Verse is alive?"*

Higginson was fascinated and challenged by what she sent him. He recognized talent in Emily's writing but considered it raw, calling it:

> *"...poetry torn up by the roots, with rain and dew and earth still clinging to them."*

He did not know what to think; so he consulted his good friend in Concord, Ralph Waldo Emerson. What did he think of the poems? Emerson wrote back that he did not think much of them.

Not wanting to crush her spirit or quell her writing efforts, yet not feeling that the poems would be publishable and appreciated by the public, Higginson finally advised her to regularize *"her rough rhythms and imperfect rhymes"* and to correct her spelling and grammar.

What had begun as a simple request for poetic appraisal had a profound effect on Emily's professional writing life. Ever true to herself, Emily rejected his advice rather than modify her work to appeal to public consumption and chose not to publish at all. She decidedly pronounced that:

"Publication is the auction of the mind of man."

It is telling of Emily's rare balance of ego and humility that rather than feeling discouraged and rejected along with her poetry, she continued to value Higginson's friendship if not his literary advice. They maintained a close correspondence for the rest of their lives. Emily still sent him more than one hundred poems over the years enclosed in letters addressed to him as, *"My safest friend"* and signed from, *"Your scholar."*

After eight years of correspondence, Higginson wished to put a face with her letters and poetry so he asked Emily to send him a picture of herself. However, she wanted to be appraised by her writing not her appearance. Rather than sending him a picture, she sent him the following reply —

"Won't this description do? ...Small like a wren; hair: bold like a chestnut; eyes: like sherry in the glass that the guest leaves."

Add to this depiction of herself to the description by others who knew her — slender in form, plain and nondescript, her most noteworthy features were her brown eyes and abundant reddish brown hair.

When Higginson finally met Emily at her home in 1870, he discovered that some relationships are best kept at a distance. He wrote to his wife of their meeting:

> *"I never was with any one who drained my nerve power so much. Without touching, she drew from me. I am glad not to live near her."*

This encounter is representative of one of the many paradoxes of Emily's life. She longed for human intimacy, but her intensity did not put people at ease. They could not meet her depth or share her poetic sense of a moment's value. Their inability to understand and relate to her contributed to her sense of loneliness and isolation.

Like many gifted people, she sensed her uniqueness early on, asking, *"What makes a few of us so different from others?"* She once wrote to Higginson, *"…all men say What to me."* To put it in today's terminology, she knew that people "just didn't get her." Even Higginson, dubious friend that he was, referred to her as his *"cracked poetess from Amherst."* Perhaps it was in the sensing of her "differentness" that she became acutely aware of her aloneness in the world. But rather than lamenting it, she embraced it and used it as strength to create her art.

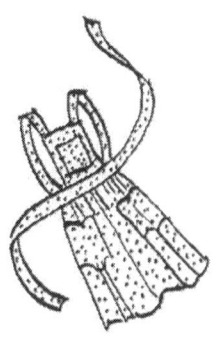

By her late twenties, she had arrived as a poet in earnest, being keenly aware of the world around her and finding divine significance in the most minute details of life. Constantly either writing or mentally composing, she wrote words she loved, words she was experimenting with and lines of poems and revisions—on bits of wrapping paper, on grocery lists, on the backs of recipes and used envelopes, in the margins of programs and on the edges of newspapers. She carried a multitude of these little scraps of paper stuffed into her apron pockets. (In England, Emily Brontë and Elizabeth Barrett Browning were carrying poetry in their apron pockets too.)

It is not clear when Emily's innate love of language and experimentation with words became a poetic vocation — an almost holy calling that required a self-imposed separation of self from society. What is clear is that, as her writing evolved, her self-concept and purpose for living evolved with it. Cloistering herself in her father's house and referring to herself as a "Wayward Nun," poetry became her service and sacrament. Writing her own sacred script, she would eventually wear only white, a symbol of her renunciation of the world to follow her holy call:

> *A solemn thing – it was – I said –*
> *A Woman – white – to be –*
> *And wear – if God should count me fit –*
> *Her blameless mystery –*
>
> *A hallowed thing – to drop a life*
> *Into the mystic well –*
> *Too plummetless – that it come back –*
> *Eternity – until –*
>
> *And then – the size of the "small" life –*
> *The Sages – call it small –*
> *Swelled – like Horizons – in my vest –*
> *And I sneered – softly – "small"!*

Lavinia called her sister's retirement from active society, *"only a happen,"* a slow process of many small separate decisions. The process was gradual, but conscious. It began as a preference for privacy and an effort to minimize the interruptions of daily life that kept her from writing. Even though she lessened her participation in daily life, she did not relinquish her connection to it. She may have limited herself to the family property, but she remained very close to her family, maintained her friendships through correspondences and avidly read the daily paper to keep abreast of local and world events. However, over the years, her seclusion fed on itself and became more phobic in nature.

In 1870, Emily wrote, *"I do not cross my father's ground to any house or town."* The national census that year listed her as *"Without Occupation"* – a common phrase used for adult daughters living at home. Emily declared otherwise:

> *For Occupation – This –*
> *The spreading wide my narrow Hands*
> *To gather Paradise –*

As she withdrew from the distractions of the outer world, she became in tune with an inner world whose immensity and sensations far exceeded anything she had experienced outside herself. *"I find ecstasy in living, the mere sense of living is joy enough…"*

> *To be alive -- is Power --*
> *Existence -- in itself --*
> *Without a further function --*
> *Omnipotence -- Enough --*

Of course, the more hermetic she became, the more curious people became about her. She began to be a local curiosity and was called *"the woman in white"* by the townsfolk of Amherst. She seemed to them like a ghostly apparition who stayed inside all day and only came out at night to walk in her garden — a solitary figure in white among the white geraniums that were her favorite flowers.

Total abandonment of organized religion fell hard on the heels of her self-imposed cloistering. In so doing, she found herself opened wide to the infinite world of the spirit, finding evidence of it in every detail of the natural world around her, *"The Supernatural is only the Natural disclosed..."*

> *Some keep the Sabbath going to Church –*
> *I keep it, staying at Home –*
> *With a Bobolink for a Chorister –*
> *And an Orchard, for a Dome –*
>
> *Some keep the Sabbath in Surplice –*
> *I just wear my Wings –*
> *And instead of tolling the Bell, for Church,*
> *Our little Sexton – sings.*
>
> *God preaches, a noted Clergyman –*
> *And the sermon is never long,*
> *So, instead of going to Heaven, at last*
> *–I'm going all along.*

Finding God manifested in the natural world, she ingeniously joined religion and nature, referring to God as the Bee, Jesus Christ as the Butterfly, and the Holy Ghost as the Breeze:

> *And one below this morning*
> *Is where the angels are --*
> *It was a short procession,*
> *The Bobolink was there --*
> *An aged Bee addressed us --*
> *And then we knelt in prayer --*
> *We trust that she was willing --*
> *We ask that we may be.*
> *Summer -- Sister -- Seraph!*
> *Let us go with thee!*
>
> *In the name of the Bee --*
> *And of the Butterfly --*
> *And of the Breeze -- Amen!*

Of the perpetual pressure to choose heavenly reward over worldly pleasure, she described her resolution to the dilemma in an earthy metaphor:

> *I cannot help esteem*
> *The Bird within the Hand*
> *Superior to the one*
> *The Bush may yield me*
> *Or may not*
> *Too late to choose again.*
> *Who has not found the heaven below*
> *Will fail of it above.*

In 1861, at age thirty-one, Emily began to experience periods of severely impaired vision. She referred to this dark time in her life, figuratively and literally, as *"terror"* in a letter to Higginson dated April 1862. In it, she refers to her poetic expressions as "singing:"

> "A terror – since September – I could tell to none – and so I sing, as the Boy does by the Burying Ground – because I am afraid."

Her *"terror"* propelled her to the height of her creativity. Terrified that her work and words would be cut short, she increased her seclusion and exploded into a fervor of poetry. In 1862, she wrote three hundred sixty-six poems—one a day. This was a dramatic increase of output in contrast to the fifty-eight poems she wrote in 1858.

During this time, she began to collect her poems into little hand sewn books called fascicles. She gathered a dozen years of work, some 1,147 poems, and honed eight hundred thirty-three of them into *"fair copies."* She discarded the rough drafts, lest they be mistaken as final copies and bound them into small volumes of five or six sheets of stationery paper that was folded and threaded at the spine.

She was sufficiently frightened enough by her deteriorating eyesight that she was twice persuaded to leave home to see an eye specialist in Boston in 1864 and 1865. The second trip lasted many months during which time she stayed with her Norcross cousins from her mother's side of the family. Far from the safe familiarities of home and forbidden to read or write by her doctor, her soul was tried to its core:

> *"It was a shutting of all the dearest ones of time, the strongest friends of the soul –BOOKS. The medical man said avaunt ye books tormentors, he also said,*

"down, thought, & plunge into her.," He might as well have said, "Eyes be blind", 'heart be still'. So I had eight weary months of Siberia.

Well do I remember the music of the welcome home....Going home I flew to the shelves and devoured the luscious passages. I thought I should tear the leaves out as I turned them."

As poets so often do, she transcribed her distress into a wonderful verse that remains one of her most popular poems:

> *There is no frigate like a book*
> *To take us lands away,*
> *Nor any coursers like a page*
> *Of prancing poetry.*
> *This traverse may the poorest take*
> *Without oppress of toll;*
> *How frugal is the chariot*
> *That bears a human soul!*

Eventually, her eye condition improved and her poetic productivity rallied, but she never produced as prolifically again.

Upon her return home Emily began a long stretch of quiet life—so removed from the world that she seemed to live outside of history. Though she read the newspaper daily, she did not mention The Great War between the North and South in her poetry. However, that did not signify indifference. The struggle between North and South resonated deeply with her. These were the years of her greatest poetic output. She was waging her own *"campaign of the interior"* against religionists, patriarchal authority and literary convention.

Meanwhile, she busied herself with caring for the garden, tending to her aging mother and baking the family bread. She made gingerbread that she lowered in a basket by a string from her upper story window to the neighborhood children waiting in the garden below.

Emily's tight little world began to unravel with the death of her father in 1874. The remoteness of his relationship with his family was caught in a moment of tragic truth when Emily's brother, Austin, leaned over the casket and kissed his dead father on the forehead, saying, *"There, Father, I never dared do that while you were living."* Although emotionally isolated, his presence was so large in his home and community that it was as if an era had passed with him. Like so many other significant Amherst events such as receptions and commencements over the years, his funeral was held on the expansive lawn of The Homestead.

Emily did not attend the funeral with the other mourners. Instead, she listened to the service from her room... the eulogy brought in by the breeze that fluttered through the lace curtains and across her wet cheeks.

The following year, 1875, offered several merciful distractions from the Dickinson family's grief. The first and most joyful event was the unplanned birth of a second son, Gilbert, to Sue and Austin, after they had been married for twenty years. The entire family was besotted with the baby and affectionately called him Little Gib. This late in life baby helped to fill the empty space in the family left by their father's passing.

Around the same time, a new character joined Emily's small cast of friends that had remained unchanged for years. Massachusetts Supreme Court Judge, Otis P. Lord, a lifelong friend of Emily's father, assumed the role of family advisor. He and his wife became regular fixtures at The Homestead.

Their presence was especially welcomed by Emily whose small world had become even more contracted when she became her mother's primary caretaker after she had suffered a paralyzing stroke. She wrote, *"Mother is lying changeless on her changeless bed."*

Her constant attendance upon Mother left her little time for anything else. *"Was there still room for poetry?"* Higginson asked her.

"I have no other playmate," she answered.

"Little wayfaring acts comprised her pursuits, and a few moments at night for books, after the rest, sleep," Higginson later surmised. Yet, Emily described her seven years of solitary service to her bedridden mother with a sense of hallowedness:

> *"When father lived I remained with him because he would miss me. Now, mother is helpless – a holier demand."*

This holy demand came with a sublime and unexpected gift of a relationship transformed:

> *"We were never intimate Mother and Children while she was our Mother, but…when she became our Child, the Affection came."*

Upon her mother's death, she wrote to Mrs. Holland:

> *"It never occurred to us that though she had not Limbs, she had soared from us unexpectedly as a summoned Bird…The dear Mother that could not walk, has flown."*

As she did when her father died, Emily listened to her mother's funeral service from the safety of her room.

In 1877, Mrs. Lord died. After her death, the affection between Judge Lord and Emily grew stronger, even blossoming into a romance. She was forty-seven years old at the time; he was sixty-five. Drafts of her letters to him speak of their mutual feelings:

> *"The creek turns into the sea at the thought of thee."*

However, when the distinguished gentleman asked her to marry him, she maintained her autonomy:

> *"But you ask the divine crust, and that would doom the bread."*

Her deep attachment to Judge Lord helped her to withstand the string of deaths of her few friends. There were five deaths in five years. It seemed as if her little world was imploding. She wrote:

> *This World did drop away*
> *As Acres from the feet*
> *Of one that leaneth from Balloon*
> *Upon an Ether street.*

The first to go was Samuel Bowles, who died in 1878. Next was his colleague, Josiah Holland, who died in 1881. The deaths of Reverend Wadsworth and her mother followed closely behind in 1882. However, in 1883, little could assuage the grief brought on by Little Gib's sudden tragic death from typhoid when he was eight years old.

The little boy, whose arrival to the world had so gladdened the sad hearts of the Dickinson clan, stopped to play in the mud with friends on a fall afternoon after school. The next day, he fell ill and did not go to school. His condition worsened during the next five days, contracting dysentery and a high fever. His parents became increasingly frantic. They attended to him night and day. Even his Aunt Emily, who never left home, ventured across the way to The Evergreens to sit by the bedside the night before her beloved nephew died. She wrote later to Mrs. Holland of the scene at the dying boy's bedside:

> *"Open the Door, open the Door, they are waiting for me," was Gilbert's sweet command in delirium.* **Who** *were waiting for him, all we possess we would give to know – Anguish at last opened it, and he ran to the little Grave at his grandparent's feet – All this and*

more, though is there more? More than Love and Death? Then tell me it's name!"

The entire family was unalterably changed by Little Gib's death. Austin became deeply despondent. Sue was embittered by her grief. Emily was so devastated that she took to her bed. She had suffered many losses, but this was beyond bearing. She never fully recovered from it. Struggling to come to terms with the pain of earthly partings, she wrote in a poem to Sue:

> *"They dropped like Flakes-,*
> *They dropped like Stars-,*
> *Like Petals from a Rose-*
> *When suddenly across the June,*
> *A wind with fingers- goes-"*

Profound love between two people, the terrible loss of one, and the hope for reunion in heaven were central themes in Emily's poetry:

> *My life closed twice before its close;*
> *It yet remains to see*
> *If immortality unveil*
> *A third event to me*
>
> *So huge, so hopeless to conceive*
> *As these that twice befell.*
> *Parting is all we know of heaven,*
> *And all we need of hell.*

Emily was exhausted and her family urged her to see a doctor. But her reclusiveness had become so phobic that she strenuously resisted, saying, *"the crisis of the sorrow of so many years is all that tires me."* She finally agreed under certain conditions. The doctor would not be allowed to enter her room but would stay in the hallway. She would open her door slightly and walk past the opening for him to view her and make his diagnosis. From this remote "examination," he rendered a general diagnosis of nervous prostration. She was most likely by now in the first stages of Bright's disease, a slow failure of the kidneys that would claim her life within three years.

She lost the companionship of Otis Lord when he died the next year, 1884. With deteriorating health and the loss of so many dear ones, she confined herself to her room for the final two years of her life. In addition to her bed, it contained a Sheraton bureau, a Franklin stove and a cherry writing table between two windows that overlooked the village cemetery. Considering Emily's rich and limitless inner world, it has been said that the end her life was *"infinity in a small room."* She began to fixate on death — pondering the intersection of time and eternity:

> *Because I could not stop for Death,*
> *He kindly stopped for me;*
> *The carriage held but just ourselves*
> *And Immortality.*
>
> *We slowly drove, he knew no haste,*
> *And I had put away*
> *My labor, and my leisure too,*
> *For his civility.*
>
> *We passed the school, where children strove*
> *At recess, in the ring;*
> *We passed the fields of gazing grain,*
> *We passed the setting sun.*

Or rather, he passed us;
The dews grew quivering and chill,
For only gossamer my gown,
My tippet only tulle.

We paused before a house that seemed
A swelling of the ground;
The roof was scarcely visible,
The cornice but a mound.

Since then 'tis centuries, and yet each
Feels shorter than the day
I first surmised the horses' heads
Were toward eternity.

She passed the summer of 1884 *"in a chair,"* but she was not too ill to keep up correspondences or to work her poetry. By November, the doctor forbade her *"book and thought."* She became even more remote even to her closest family members. Death was ever present in her mind.

In April, 1886, confined to her bed, she presciently wrote to Higginson, *"There is no trumpet like the Tomb."* One month later in May, feeling the pull of the other side, she penned a peaceful and prophetic note to her Norcross cousins that seems to indicate that she had finally resolved her unremitting questions concerning God, her place in this world and the world to come:

"*Little Cousins,*

Called back.

Emily"

Death came quietly to the quiet poet who had lived a quiet life. On Thursday, May 13, 1886, Emily silently slipped into unconsciousness at ten in the morning. Vinnie sent for Austin and they began the death watch for their sister. On Friday, still unconscious, she lapsed into the rattled breathing that those in the Victorian Age knew signaled impending death. On Saturday, May 15, Austin wrote in his diary:

> *"It was settled before morning broke that Emily would not wake again this side. The day was awful. She ceased to breathe that terrible breathing just before the whistles sounded for six."*

Emily Elizabeth Dickinson was fifty-five years of age.

On Tuesday, May 18, Emily's obituary appeared on the editorial page of "The Springfield Republican," – a poignant eulogy penned by dearest friend and sister-in-law, Sue. It would be the first of countless treatises on the life of this intriguing and brilliant woman of "Myth and Shadow:"

> *"The death of Miss Emily Dickinson, daughter of the late Edward Dickinson, at Amherst on Saturday, makes another sad inroad on the small circle so long occupying the family mansion... Very few in the village, except among the older inhabitants, knew Miss Emily personally, although the facts of her seclusion and her intellectual brilliancy were familiar Amherst traditions... As she passed on in life, her sensitive nature shrank from much personal contact with the world, and more and more turned to her own large wealth of individual resources for companionship... Not disappointed with the world, not an invalid until*

the past two years, not from any lack of sympathy, not because she was insufficient for any mental work or social career – her endowments being so exceptional – but the "mesh of her soul"… was too rare, and the sacred quiet of her own home proved the fit atmosphere for her worth and work…

…To her, life was rich and all aglow with God and immortality. With no creed, no formulated faith, hardly knowing the names of dogmas, she walked this life with a gentleness and reverence of old saints. With the firm step of martyrs who sing while they suffer."

Emily was buried the next day, Wednesday, May 19, 1886. In accordance with her wishes not to have a funeral service in the church, a small group gathered at The Homestead. Many of them had not seen her face in twenty-five years. Her lifelong friend and correspondent, Thomas Higginson, noted in his diary:

"She… looked 30, not a gray hair or wrinkle, & perfect peace on the beautiful brow."

Emily rested in a white casket strewn with vibrant violets. She was dressed in the simple white dress she had worn in life. Lavinia pinned a small corsage of violets to her collar and put two heliotropes in her hand to *"take to Judge Lord."*

During the service, Higginson read aloud the poem, "No Coward Soul is Mine," by that other Emily, called Brontë, who had lived across the ocean and also searched for God in His Heaven but had instead found Heaven in Earth.

God's Singers

Traditionally in Amherst, funeral processions passed up Main Street, turning right onto North Pleasant to enter into West Street Cemetery. However, in keeping with Emily's wishes, her casket was carried out the back door, through the yard, between the hedges, and across the meadow *"full of buttercups and violet & wild geranium"* into the graveyard where she was laid on a cradle of pine boughs to be buried next to her parents.

The bright May air, heavy with the pungent scent of apple blossoms, vibrated with the drone of bees. Birds and butterflies flitted through the sun's rays. It seemed to be a Dickinson poem incarnate.

Austin inscribed Emily's tombstone with her own words—a message of unvarnished simplicity in which she revealed her final reconciliation with God:

"Called Back."

Emily As A Poet

Now Lavinia was left alone at the The Homestead. Though the big house must have already been a quiet one, having been inhabited by two spinster sisters who highly prized their privacy, one being a recluse, there is something to be said for having the mere presence of another person nearby. Even if the presence is distant and quiet, it still eases the loneliness in one's soul. What Lavinia could not have known in those early empty days without Emily was that she would come to know her sister better in death than she ever had in life. When she finally summoned enough emotional strength to go through her dead sister's belongings, she was astonished to discover a treasure trove of words beyond her imagining. Emily's poetry plunged Vinnie into her sister's soul after death in a way that had been denied her in life. Vinnie had known that Emily had a penchant for words, but, evidently, her penchant for privacy was even greater. She never knew that Emily's predilection for words went beyond whim to the divine call of poet.

She found more than eight hundred poems gathered into forty fascicles. Nearly four hundred more poems were arranged in the manner of booklets, though not yet bound—along with miscellaneous fair copies, semi-final drafts, and numerous worksheet drafts written on odds and ends of paper. Recognizing her sister's genius, she excitedly shared her findings with her sister-in-law, Sue. The two women resolved to get Emily's work into print.

They first consulted Thomas Wentworth Higginson, Emily's longtime correspondent and friend—the literary publicist who had discouraged her from publishing during her lifetime.   Now that Emily was no longer alive to object, he edited the poems to meet accepted standards of meter and rhyme with the assistance of Mabel Loomis Todd of Amherst College. They chose one hundred fourteen poems for Emily's first published volume of poetry in 1890.

Even with conventional editing, reviewers were still hostile. But the reading public was ready for Emily Dickinson. When they demanded more, Mrs. Todd brought out two more volumes of poetry and two volumes of letters.

As Emily's work grew in popularity and familiarity, people began to surface with poems Emily had given them, some anonymously, saying, "This looks like Emily Dickinson."   In time, a total of about 1,775 poems attributed to her were published.

For nearly a century, Emily's work appeared sporadically in print. Emily's niece, Martha Dickinson Bianchi, published volumes in 1914, 1929 and 1932. Another book was published in 1945, three more volumes in 1955 and another in 1960.

In 1955, Thomas Johnson began the long overdue restoration of Emily's poems as she intended them. By restoring the dashes and capital letters where she had written them, he returned the poetry to its original form in his three volumes, _The Poems of Emily Dickinson_, (Belknap Press of Harvard University Press).

But there was still more work of recovery to be done. It was not until 1981 that Emily's poems were published in their original fascicle form with the publication of Franklin's _Manuscript Book of Emily Dickinson_.   Using such evidence as stationery imperfections, smudge patterns, and puncture marks where the poet's needle had pierced the paper to bind them more than a hundred years earlier, Franklin restored Emily's poems to their original fascicle form for the first time since Lavinia's initial discovery. This restoration of Emily's work in its original form ushered in a new era of Dickinson scholarship.

Remarkably, in 1993, five hundred new poems showed up in print from University of Tennessee professor, William H. Shurr. Having taught Dickinson classes for twenty years, he began to see lines, patterns, and rhythms in her letters. Taking a phrase from one letter here and another phrase from another letter there, he extracted five hundred new poems from her letters and published <u>New Poems by Emily Dickinson</u>, University of North Carolina Press. Professor Shurr explained his process by referring, again, to poetry as song, *"Her meters are like beautiful songs. As I read her letters, they just start singing like her poems."*

Even though she lived and wrote during the nineteenth century, so much of Emily's work has been published in the twentieth century that not only has she been classed as a modern poet, but her work stands out as the turning point for the modernization of the art of poetry. Indeed, she redefined the parameters of poetry as we know it today. Arlo Bates, a late nineteenth century Boston critic, observed that, *"it is to be judged as if it were a new species of art."*

Emily Dickinson lived the way she wrote, discarding the inessentials of distraction in order to dwell at the heart's core where the pure essence of truth exists. She sought to commune with the divine not from extremity but from living an examined life. She had no interest in wasting her time with any custom, convention, tradition or rule in both living and writing that would detract from the truth of a matter.

She wrote, *"I dwell in possibility."* For her, paradoxically, possibility was attained in limiting her world. She rejected the church, finding it superfluous to divine truth. She rejected sociability, finding it a hindrance to the true communion of individual souls. She rejected life beyond her home doors, finding it unnecessary to leave the familiar to experience the ecstatic:

> *I dwell in Possibility--*
> *A fairer House than Prose--*
> *More numerous of Windows--*
> *Superior--for Doors--*
>
> *Of Chambers as the Cedars--*
> *Impregnable of Eye--*
> *And for an Everlasting Roof*
> *The Gambrels of the Sky--*
>
> *Of Visitors--the fairest--*
> *For Occupation--This--*
> *The spreading wide my narrow Hands*
> *To gather Paradise--*

She learned to tinker with meter when she discovered that the words of one hymn can be sung to the music of another. Using hymn patterns, she innovated on the meters of her poetry in unique ways, using simple phrases.

From experimenting with meter, she began to stretch, twist and bend words to her service. Adjectives and verbs may be used as nouns:

We talk in careless – and in loss.

The Possible's slow fuse is lit by the Imagination.

She did not exist to serve language; language existed to serve her! She dropped the rules of grammar, capitalizing nouns and conjunctions, not only for emphasis but seemingly at random, to suit her mood. She loved to use dashes — often using them to replace commas and periods. Perhaps they seemed more fluid to her, in keeping with the way her thoughts linked up one with another.

She was the master of expressing the inexpressible by reducing it down to the finest particle, distilling it to its essence. She could find the ocean in a drop of water, the beach in a grain of sand, God's word in the buzz of a bee. Henry W. Wells explained it best when he wrote:

> *"Life is simplified, explained, and reduced to its essence by interpreting the vast whole in relation to the minute particle."*

She was the ultimate minimalist in her capacity to compress language and thought. Valuing silence as well as sound, the pauses speak as loudly as the words in her elliptical verse. Using bursts of language to capture explosions of thought or ideas, she was the pioneer of the sound byte.

Emily Line by Line

Forever is composed of nows.

Fortune befriends the bold.

Anger as soon as fed is dead – 'Tis starving makes it fat.

Beauty is not caused. It is.

Water, is taught by thirst.

Behavior is what a man does, not what he thinks, feels, or believes.

Celebrity is the chastisement of merit and the punishment of talent.

Fame is a fickle food upon a shifting plate.

Whenever a thing is done for the first time, it releases a little demon.

Irony and humor is often present:

Truth is so rare, that it is delightful to tell it.

Tell the truth, but tell it slant.

*Surgeons must be very careful, when they take the knife!
Underneath their fine incisions, stirs the Culprit – Life!*

*That it will never come again
Is what makes life so sweet.*

Emily Dickinson

To make a prairie it takes a clover and one bee,
One clover, and a bee, And revery.
The revery alone will do, If bees are few.

Especially when ruminating on the question of God:

Faith is Doubt.

> *Faith is a fine invention*
> *For gentlemen who see;*
> *But microscopes are prudent*
> *In an emergency.*

They say that God is everywhere, and yet we always think of Him as somewhat of a recluse.

> *"Heavenly Father" -- take to thee*
> *The supreme iniquity*
> *Fashioned by thy candid Hand*
> *In a moment contraband --*
>
> *Though to trust us seems to us*
> *More respectful –*
> *"We are Dust" --*
> *We apologize to thee*
> *For thine own Duplicity.*

She made the abstract tangible by giving it concrete imagery. Here, she uses imperfect rather than exact rhyme such as "soul, and all:"

> *Hope is the thing with feathers-*
> *That perches in the soul-*
> *And sings the tune without the words-*
> *And never stops- at all –*

Adept at recognizing eternity in the actual, she substantiated a happening by giving it physical attributes:

> *I'll tell you how the sun rose,*
> *A ribbon at a time.*
> *The steeples swam in amethyst,*
> *The news like squirrels ran.*
> *The hills untied their bonnets,*
> *The bobolinks begun.*
> *Then I said softly to myself,*
> *"That must have been the sun!"*

> *Presentiment is that long shadow on the lawn*
> *Indicative that suns go down;*
> *The notice to the startled grass*
> *That darkness is about to pass.*

She actualized and materialized ideas:

> *I felt a cleaving in my mind*
> *As if my brain had split;*
> *I tried to match it, seam by seam,*
> *But could not make them fit.*

The thought behind I strove to join
Unto the thought before,
But sequence raveled out of reach
Like balls upon a floor.

She found the anticipation of an event to be more ecstatic than the event itself. For her, the joy was in the chase, not in the catch. A recurrent theme was one of anticipating the goal, not achieving the goal.

Arriving toward arrival:

To possess is past the instant.

Not knowing when the dawn will come I open every door.

The soul should always stand ajar, ready to welcome the ecstatic experience.

Success is counted sweetest
By those who ne'er succeed.
To comprehend a nectar
Requires sorest need.

Not one of all the purple host
Who took the flag to-day
Can tell the definition
So clear, of victory,

As he, defeated, dying,
On whose forbidden ear
The distant strains of triumph
Break, agonized and clear.

We never know how high we are
Till we are called to rise;
And then, if we are true to plan,
Our statures touch the skies.

The heroism we recite
Would be a daily thing,
Did not ourselves the cubits warp
For fear to be a king.

Nature was a faithful muse — flowers, birds and bees offered abundant inspiration:

The robin's my criterion for tune.
Because I grow
Where robins do
But were I cuckoo born
I swear by him
The ode familiar
Rules the noon
The buttercup's my whim for bloom
Because, we're orchard sprung
But were I Britain born,
I'd daisies spurn
None but the nut October fit
Because, through dropping it
The seasons flit ---I'm taught
Without the snow's tableau winter
Were lie – to me –
Because I see – New Englandly –
The Queen, discerns like me–
Provincially –

Emily Dickinson

*A Bird came down the Walk —
He did not know I saw —
He bit an angle-worm in halves
And ate the fellow, raw,*

*And then he drank a Dew
From a convenient Grass,
And then hopped sidewise to the Wall
To let a Beetle pass —*

*He glanced with rapid eyes
That hurried all abroad —
They looked like frightened Beads, I thought —
He stirred his velvet head*

*Like one in danger, Cautious,
I offered him a Crumb,
And he unrolled his feathers
And rowed him softer home —*

*Than Oars divide the Ocean,
Too silver for a seam —
Or Butterflies, off Banks of Noon,
Leap, splashless as they swim.*

God's Singers

Will there really be a "Morning"?
Is there such a thing as "Day"?
Could I see it from the mountains
If I were as tall as they?

Has it feet like Water lilies?
Has it feathers like a Bird?
Is it brought from famous countries
Of which I have never heard?

Oh some Scholar! Oh some Sailor!
Oh some Wise Men from the skies!
Please to tell a little Pilgrim
Where the place called "Morning" lies!

I'M nobody! Who are you?
Are you nobody, too?
Then there's a pair of us – don't tell!
They'd banish us, you know.

How dreary - to be - somebody!
How public - like a frog -
To tell your name - the livelong June -
To an admiring bog!

Emily Dickinson

A little madness in the Spring
Is wholesome even for the King,
But God be with the Clown,
Who ponders this tremendous scene –
This whole experiment of green,
As if it were his own.

The search to know God and understand the paradoxical nature of the Divine was an omnipresent theme in her poetry until the end of her life:

I cannot see my soul but I know 'tis there.

I shall know why, when time is over,
And I have ceased to wonder why;
Christ will explain each separate anguish
In the fair schoolroom of the sky.

When he tells us about his Father, we distrust him.
When he shows us his Home, we turn away,
But when he confides to us that he is acquainted with grief,
We listen, For that is also an acquaintance of our own.

I know that he exists
Somewhere- in Silence
He has hid his rare life
From our gross eyes.

At least to pray is left is left
Oh Jesus in the Air
I know not which thy chamber is –
I'm knocking everywhere.

God's Singers

I never saw a moor;
I never saw the sea;
Yet know I how the heather looks,
And what a wave must be.

I never spoke with God,
Nor visited in heaven;
Yet certain am I of the spot
As if the chart were given.

Love's Baptism

I'm ceded, I've stopped being theirs;
The name they dropped upon my face
With water, in the country church,
Is finished using now,
And they can put it with my dolls,
My childhood, and the string of spools
I've finished threading too.

Emily Dickinson

Baptized before without the choice,
But this time consciously, of grace
Unto supremest name,
Called to my full, the crescent dropped,
Existence's whole arc filled up
With one small diadem.

My second rank, too small the first,
Crowned, crowing on my father's breast,
A half unconscious queen;
But this time, adequate, erect,
With will to choose or to reject.
And I choose -- just a throne.

Emily Dickinson lived a life of paradox while she struggled to make sense of the paradoxical nature of life. Yet, perhaps the greatest paradox of all occurred after Emily's death. From this great Dickinson clan of Pilgrims, Pioneers, Revolutionaries, Founders, Judges and Lawyers—it is the shy, reclusive, enigmatic woman, who penned poems in her pantry and stuffed them in her apron pockets that history remembers. Emily Dickinson is the name that has become household. It is her words that will be forever on our lips:

If I can stop one heart from breaking,
I shall not live in vain;
If I can ease one life the aching,
Or cool one pain,
Or help one fainting robin
Unto his nest again,
I shall not live in vain.

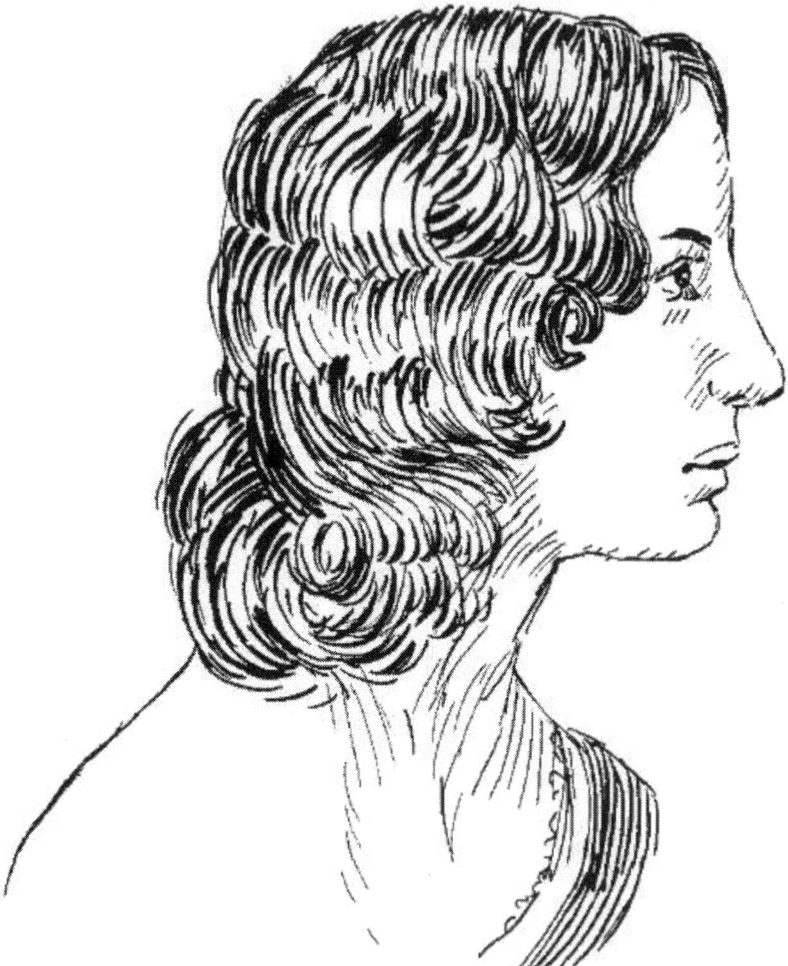

Emily Jane Brontë
1818 – 1848

"Oh God, my poor children," moaned Maria Brontë with her last breath in the upper room of the cold stone house on the treeless hill beside the graveyard. Its stone floors were icy and cold. Its curtainless windows were icy and cold. Maria was icy and cold. The chilling wind that ceaselessly battered the house, rattled the panes and sobbed as if to mark her passing, and the cold gravestones below silently beckoned her to join them.

Six *"spiritless"* little ones huddled close together in a dark lower room:

> *"grave and silent beyond their years…[one] would not have known there was a child in the house, they were such still, noiseless creatures."*

Not even the baby, Anne, not yet two years old, made a sound in her oldest sister Maria's arms. The six year old explained to the rest of them that their mother was dying. The little Brontë's — Elizabeth, Charlotte, Branwell, and Emily — were used to listening to Maria. It was she who led them on their long rambles across the heathered moors above their house in all weather. It was she who read the newspaper to them (they did not have children's books) in quiet undertones so as not to disturb their parents. If they did not understand the words, "mother is dying," they surely sensed impending disaster.

Their father, Patrick Brontë, though still living, was — like all else — icy and cold. He regarded his children as a drain on his wife and an interruption to his comfort.

The stern evangelist attempted to discharge his anxieties by firing his pistol from the kitchen door at the church tower across the graveyard on frosty mornings.

Patrick Brontë, originally Prunty, was born on St. Patrick's Day, 1777, in a two room thatched cottage in County Down, Ireland. He shared these two rooms with his parents, Hugh and Alice, and his four brothers and five sisters. Along with twelve people in these two rooms were two books, *The Bible* and *Pilgrim's Progress*. Patrick read and reread them until he knew them by heart.

By the time he was twenty-two, he had worked as a farm hand, a blacksmith and a weaver. With his meager earnings, he scraped together enough money to buy Milton's *Paradise Lost*, which he also memorized. Finally, he escaped the manual labor he was born to and landed employment as a schoolteacher.

A wealthy university educated Reverend Tighe took a liking to the fiery carrot-topped Patrick and convinced him that his true calling was to be a servant of God. Without Tighe's help, Patrick would have never gotten into St. John's, Tighe's own college in England, to become an ordained minister in the Anglican Church.

When Patrick arrived in England, he changed his name to distance himself from his early poverty. Brontë looked and sounded more refined and would be more acceptable in the English school where he would become the minister, author and poet that he knew he could be. He hid his Irish background and never returned to Ireland.

After a dozen years as an assistant clergyman, Patrick secured a senior clergyman position in Dewsbury, Yorkshire. It was here that he met Maria Branwell, age thirty, at the home of a friend. The friend was Maria's cousin who she was visiting from Penzance. From the surprisingly frank love letters that flew between them, it appears that it was love at first sight. Patrick's vocation as an impoverished clergyman did not in the least dampen Maria's ardor for him; on the contrary, it seemed to enhance it. A woman of high ideals, she believed that poverty enhanced the religious seeker's quest for godliness. She espoused this idea in a way that only a person who had never experienced poverty could. The two idealists were engaged just one month after they met and wed three months later. They were married just nine years before Maria died.

In the first seven years of her marriage, she bore six children. When our poet, Emily, was born, the fifth of six children, her oldest sister was just four years and three months old.

- 1814 – Maria
- 1815 – Elizabeth
- 1816 – Charlotte
- 1817 – Branwell
- 1818 – Emily
- 1820 – Anne

When baby Anne was just four months old, Patrick took over the leadership of a cantankerous little parish in a remote part of Yorkshire that had chased out their previous curate. When the Brontë family arrived on a late afternoon in April 1820, with seven carts containing their worldly possessions, their reception from the inhabitants of Haworth was as cold as the treeless moor their town was built upon. The inmates of Haworth were sour for good reason. It was one of the unhealthiest places in England. Its main street was built on a hillside so steep that the cobblestones in the town had to be lain sideways to give the horses traction. The houses on either side sat so close together that they almost looked like they were clinging to each other for support to keep from sliding down the incline. Beyond the main street was a mix of stone mills and stone cottages closely scattered along the low rocky moors whose earth was unfit for a garden or a tree.

Six thousand people, most of whom worked in the textile industry, were crammed into this meager collection of stone structures along with their animals and 1200 handlooms. They burned charcoal stoves day and night to keep the wool at the right temperature for processing.

Grey on grey on grey. Grey stone houses erupting from the grey ground like uneven blemishes, puffing out grey charcoal smoke against a grey sky, wet with a grey drizzle sapping sunshine and spirit from the grey faced tenants. One element, human or not, was hardly distinguishable from another. No wonder the town's four pubs, all a stone's throw from each other did a brisk business.

But the greatest blight on Haworth was its lack of a proper sewage system. Communal privies were shared by dozens of families whose refuse drained in open channels down the cobblestone streets as well as behind and between the houses. These open drains led to cesspools and dung heaps at the bottom of the hill that stunk and bred disease. Just yards away from these cesspools were the taps for the supply of water for nearby houses.

The mortality rate for the inhabitants of Haworth was staggeringly high. Nearly half of the children died before they reached the age of six. The average age of death was at times as low as nineteen years old. Two souls a week were sent to the overcrowded graveyard at the edge of town. Perhaps that is why Haworth so desperately needed a new vicar. He would have regular work of sending souls to God. It was to this bleak blight of a place that Patrick brought his family. He would earn one hundred eighty pounds a year in addition to being provided a home, the Parsonage.

The Parsonage sat like a silent sentinel on its own hill next to the town. Mrs. Gaskell, family friend and first Brontë biographer, wrote of it:

"the wild vehemence of the wind, it goes piping and wailing and sobbing round the square unsheltered house in a very strange unearthly way."

Separating the house from Haworth was a graveyard overly stuffed with great grey slabs and headstones that jutted and leaned in every conceivable direction. They were jammed so close together that hardly a weed could grow between the monuments. This overcrowding, along with the custom of covering the graves with large flat stones, directly contributed to the chronic ill health of the Brontë family. The over abundance of stone assured that nothing could grow over the graves to assist in the decomposition process. Thus the ground was chronically contaminated with unresolved decomposition. It was into this ground that the Brontë well was sunk. Water drawn from this well had a peculiar film on its surface. Having never known anything otherwise, the dwellers of the Parsonage never questioned its presence and daily drank their deaths.

The Parsonage was not part of the community. The citizenry of Haworth were a *"close"* group, hostile to strangers. They were an illiterate bunch of weavers and woolcombers who had most likely never traveled more than ten miles from home, and who spoke with a thick brogue that rendered them nearly incomprehensible to outsiders. As far as they were concerned, the Brontës may as well have been from another planet, being schooled and coming from far off places like Ireland and Cornwall. Perhaps the Reverend Brontë did as well as he did in Haworth because he shared their anti-social nature. As one of them put it, *"he minds his own business, and ne'er troubles himself with ours."*

Just beyond the house rose the *"long low moors, dark little heaths, shut in valleys where a stream waters here or there a fringe of stunted copse."* They undulated endlessly like waves of an earthy ocean as far as the eye could see. But neither did the Parsonage belong to the moors. It was in a twilight zone between two worlds. On one side of the house was the suffering refuse of humanity and death. On the other side was the boundless, open, wild, untamed possibility of the natural world. When the little Brontë's ventured from the Parsonage, it was never in the direction of town. No wonder they chose to go in the direction they did.

Six little children, the older ones helping the younger ones still plump with toddlerhood, ventured out alone to roam the wild moors, in all weather, with the same curiosity and abandon as the creatures native to it. There was no adult nearby to remind them that they were not of this world, but only visitors in it. With no one to tell them, "don't touch that, don't go there, hurry up, it's time to go," they explored and examined, at childhood's pace—heath and heather, fell fields and leas, split by silver streams and broken by craggy bluffs. *"Every moss, every flower, every tint and form were noted and enjoyed."* They embraced every breeze, watched lapwings in flight, or observed the scurrying of a wood mouse for as long as their hearts delighted — returning to the Parsonage sodden and muddy, baptized by earth, bonded as her own. In later years, Charlotte wrote:

> *"It is only higher up, deep in amongst the ridges of the moors, that Imagination can find rest for the sole of his foot; and even if she find it there she must be a solitude loving raven, no gentle dove."*

To the Brontë children, the Parsonage in its no man's land was the home that offered refuge from a frightening and unfriendly world that they did not understand. In her poem, "A Little While, A Little While," the grown up Emily sees her home for the cold and barren place it is. But she loves it; and it is her love for it that makes it beautiful and dear:

Emily Brontë

There is a spot, mid barren hills,
Where winter howls, and driving rain;
But if the dreary tempest chills,
There is a light that warms again.

The house is old, the trees are bare,
Moonless above bends twilight's dome;
But what on earth is half so dear,
So longed for, as the hearth of home?

The mute bird sitting on the stone,
The dank moss dripping from the wall,
The thorn-trees gaunt, the walks o'ergrown,
I love them, how I love them all!

Emily Brontë was the most reclusive and home loving of all our poets. But her true love and natural habitat was the Yorkshire moors — that wild expanse just beyond her home. To her the moors were not bleak or barren or desolate. Their spare beauty transcended human comforts, which were few. The moors were mother to motherless Emily. They nurtured her like a mother nurtures her child, and she responded to them with a pagan spirit. Emily was Charlotte's *"solitude loving raven, no gentle dove."* She called her sister *"native and nursling of the moors."*

When Emily's mother died, either of cancer or of a chronic infection related to multiple pregnancies, she was only three years old. She had no memory of her. The next closest thing she had to a mother figure was her oldest sister, Maria, only six, who nevertheless understood that she was the only one left to love her five little siblings. It certainly was not Papa, who woke the house every morning with gunshot. And it certainly was not Aunt Bran who had come to take care of mother when she was sick. Aunt Bran loathed everything around her, the climate, the countryside, the town. And she seemed on the edge of loathing the tiny inmates of the Parsonage as well.

Patrick had talked her into staying until he found a new wife and mother for his children. But after four unsuccessful proposals in three years time, Patrick begrudgingly persuaded her to stay. She took the larger upstairs bedroom with the fireplace in which her sister had died. She scarcely stirred from it for the next twenty years. She even took her dinner in solitude in her room while her brother-in-law took his meals in solitude in his study. This left the Brontë children to eat their meals alone in the kitchen. With no adult interaction, and no one to make sure they ate their vegetables first and saved their apple pudding for last, they all became picky, erratic eaters. After dinner, they all slept in the tiny, unheated *"children's study"* on camp beds that were folded up during the day. The Brontë children belonged to themselves… no mother, no father, no neighbors, no school, no children's books or toys.

When Aunt did issue from her room, her wooden clogs clacking on the stone floors and echoing all over the house, she ruled with a regimentation that agreed very well with Patrick's sensibilities. Lessons, baking, prayers, sweeping, stitching-- the hours were so tightly structured the same every day that you could set your clock by them. In later years, the only tribute the Brontë sisters could pay to their Bran was that she instilled within them a sense of duty, order and punctuality.

Aunt was so cold and commanding that she dismissed the two servant girls who had been with the family for years. However, they were replaced with a crusty middle aged matron from the village named Tabby who could hold her own with Aunt Bran. She was a hardened Haworth inhabitant, but not so hard that there was not room in her heart for the Brontë orphans. There were no demonstrations of tender affection, but underneath her rough and simple exterior, she loved them and they knew it. Tabby was their one link with town folk and town ways. She told old time tales in her old time brogue of days long past. She even told of seeing fairies down by the *"beck"* on moonlit nights. Tabby brought a wee bit o' magic to the austere, preternaturally mature world of the Brontë orphans.

For all their regimented days, the children's education was haphazard at best. They received occasional lessons from their father in history, geography and arithmetic, but it was needlework (a requirement of Victorian women) that was taught most consistently by Aunt Bran. Before they could even read or write, the girls were given workboxes that contained their needles, thimbles and floss. They learned their alphabet by stitching it.

While they stitched, they would by turns take a break to read to the others, though not from children's books, as there were none. They read from their father's library. Their favorites were Shakespeare, Byron, Wordsworth, Coleridge and Shelley. Their two great favorites were the same as their father's, Milton's <u>Paradise Lost</u> and Bunyan's <u>Pilgrim's Progress</u>. And they read the daily paper. Reading and writing became their escape from the daily routines and chores.

However haphazard his lessons were, the education of his daughters was, in fact, Patrick's chief concern. They were in a precarious position. He was aware that he did not own their home. If anything happened to him, they would be turned out into a world that made poor provision for orphans. He also had no money to provide dowries; consequently, their chances of marriage were greatly weakened. If his daughters found themselves in the world with no home, no money or no husbands, they would need to be able to either teach school or be governesses. Both of these professions had little respect and paid scanty wages, but the only other option was destitution—begging or the workhouse.

He must have been relieved to find The Clergy Daughters' School, a semi-charitable institution for girls such as his, fifty-four miles away from Haworth at Cowan Bridge. His two eldest girls, Maria and Elizabeth, aged nine and ten, were the first to go in July 1824. Charlotte and Emily's enrollment were delayed because they were sick with whooping cough and measles. By August, Charlotte, age eight, joined her sisters. Emily, age six, followed in November.

When Patrick took his first three daughters to the school, he was satisfied enough with the facility; so he did not escort Emily there himself. Instead he sent her on in a carriage with a family friend. Perhaps if he had taken Emily as well, he may have been able to discover the truth about the hellish place in which he had placed his little girls-- then again, maybe not. It is incredible to the modern mind that the founder of the school, William Carus Wilson, got away with what he did for as long as he did without arousing suspicion. Did anyone inquire about the children's schedule or their diet? Did not one parent review any class texts and books used by the school? Did they not interview any teachers, students or parents? It was a different world then, but when faced with situations as extreme as this, it is hard not to judge it by our current standards.

The school day started at six a.m. in their unheated dormitory. Before they could wash their faces on cold mornings, they had to break the ice in their wash basins to get to the frigid water below. Shivering, they pulled on their black stockings, purple merino dresses and brown pinafores. It did not take them long to pull a comb through their hair as it was shorn off, as soon as they arrived at the school. Between seven and eight, they prayed, read the Bible, memorized verses and sang hymns. Then, they ate a breakfast of porridge and milk before tending to their lessons until noon. Between noon and one, they exercised, which consisted of strenuous walking, no games. They would lunch on boiled beef and a vegetable before three more hours of lessons. Dinner at five was dry bread and milk. Next, the older girls did two more hours of lessons until eight, when they got a bit more milk and dry bread before bed.

What little food the girls received was tainted, spoiled and burnt. The milk was sour and lumpy, the porridge was burnt, the fatty meat was rotten, and puddings were made with water taken from the rain barrel, full of dust, bugs and dead leaves. The girls were hungry enough that they greedily grabbed whatever food they could, however nauseating it was. Some of the bigger girls even took food out of the little ones' bowls, leaving them weak and empty handed.

The texts that the children studied from were produced by Wilson himself. He aimed to save their wicked young souls while teaching them to read. His beginning reader was called *The Child's First Tales*. It began with a woodcut illustration of a man hanging from the gallows. Underneath, in easy to read one syllable words, was, "Look there! Do you see a man hung by the neck?" Another tale told the story of a three year old little girl who did not mind her mother. It concluded with, "All at once God struck her dead…Where is she now? We know that bad girls go to Hell." All of Wilson's text's central themes were torture, death, hellfire and damnation. These were the only "children's books" that the Brontë girls ever read.

Daily deprivation and menacing textbooks were the methods that Wilson used to fulfill his mission to his young charges-- subject them to suffering in order to inure them to all carnal needs and desires and terrorize them into submissive obedience.

The sensitive and gentle Maria Brontë, surrogate mother to her sisters and brother, was a bright child, but she was also prone to day dreaming and untidiness. (Perhaps she was day dreaming about food and too weak to be neat.) She was mercilessly hounded by one of the school's sadistic teachers. After six months of incarceration at Cowan Bridge, she was in permanent decline with tuberculosis — undoubtedly brought on from being weakened by starvation and exposure. She was sent home, a skeletal remnant of her former self, hollow-eyed and wasted. She died three weeks later in the same bed in which her mother had died. She was eleven years old.

Shockingly, Patrick did not withdraw his other daughters from this institution until the school sent his second daughter, Elizabeth, home three months later to die in the same condition as her sister.

Now Emily, Charlotte, Branwell and Anne not only had a mother buried beneath the stone church floor, they had two sisters, cold and silent, there as well. Losing Maria, the closest thing to a mother any of them had, shattered what little was left of any sense of love and security in the young Brontë's world. Emily, now seven years old became extremely fearful and withdrawn. She equated leaving home and being in contact with people other than her immediate family with deprivation and death. Life meant loss upon loss that was beyond her control. It would become a major theme in her writing.

The family pulled together in shared grief and mourning that summer. But by the first frost of fall, Aunt had returned to her room, and Papa had returned to his study. The four children who were left drew an even tighter imaginary circle around themselves than before. Emily and Charlotte huddled together each night in the same small foldable cot for warmth and comfort in the unheated children's study. Winter passed in a long unbroken string of leaden days. But the following summer, a simple gift enabled them to weave the frayed, hanging threads of their lives into a *"web of sunny air."*

In June 1826, Patrick Brontë went to a clergyman's conference in Leeds, and he came home bearing gifts for his children: a set of ninepins for Charlotte, a toy village for Emily, a doll for Anne, and a set of toy soldiers for Branwell. Happy as the girls were with their toys, it was Branwell's soldiers that possessed the imaginations of all the children. Charlotte recounts the morning that the wondrous toy soldiers arrived:

> *"Papa bought Branwell some wooden soldiers at Leeds. When Papa came home it was night, and we were in*

> *bed, so next morning Branwell came to our door with a box of soldiers. Emily and I jumped out of bed and I snatched one and exclaimed, "This is the Duke of Wellington! This shall be the duke!" When I had said this Emily likewise took up one and said it should be hers; when Anne came down she said one should be hers."*

Branwell named his hero Bonaparte. Emily and Anne chose the arctic explorers Captain Edward Parry and Captain John Ross as their heroes. All their imaginary heroes were taken from the real life people they had been reading about, or had been read to them, in the newspapers since they were toddlers. They coupled the inspiration from current day heroes with all the classics they had devoured — Milton, Bunyan, Scott, Byron, Wordsworth, Coleridge, and Southey — and came up with a feast for the imagination that filled the empty spaces in their lives.

They used every resource at hand to create complex epic sagas. It began with the "Young Men" who set sail in 1793 on the seventy-four gun warship Invincible with a crew of *"twelve men, everyone healthy and stout and in the best temper."* The Invincible and its heroes were protected by four Chief Genii — Branni (Branwell), Talli (Charlotte), Emmii (Emily), and Annii (Anne) — who saw them safely through storms and other disasters at sea until they reached the West Coast of Africa.

As soon as the "Twelves" stepped ashore, they were attacked by the native "Ashantees," embodied by Charlotte's set of ninepins. After vanquishing the Aboriginals, they colonized the continent in the finest English empire building fashion. The "Twelves" divided the conquered territory into four kingdoms —

Wellington's Land, Parry's Land, Ross's Land and Napoleon's Land (unaccountably called Sneaky's Land). These kingdoms made up the Glass Town Confederacy of which Branwell drew up a detailed map.

From here, the alter egos of Brontë children explored and discovered wild unknown lands, encountered strange cultures and animals, built palaces, including a Palace of Instruction for one thousand pupils. Territories were annexed; wars were fought in which the heroes killed thousands with impunity as everything could always be *"made alive again."* In the Glass Town Confederacy, the sun always shone, rivers and lakes sparkled with clear water, and snow capped mountains crested the horizon. It was all very far away from Haworth.

This imaginary world gives a clear picture of the voids in the children's lives that they were trying to fill. Their characters or alter egos endowed the children with powers both natural and supernatural. To begin with, their vessel was Invincible. They could not fail. Their alter egos were free agents who had the power to go where they wanted, when they wanted. Most importantly, each adventurer was protected by a Genii who had the power to make everything *"alive again."* There was no death.

Their plays became so complex that after three years, they began to document everything. They published a monthly magazine called "The Young Men's Blackwood's Magazine," modeled after their favorite family periodical "Blackwood's." They wrote political and social histories of the Glass Town Confederacy chronicling all the details of civilization building — conquests, treaties, aristocratic high life, love affairs in tiny books of their own making. Some of the booklets were so diminutive they were only slightly larger than a postage stamp. These tiny tomes with their microscopic printing contained the history of entire civilizations, including many features such as adventures, book reviews, political commentary, illustrations and even letters to the editor.

They created their books in miniature fashion because paper was scarce, but it also seemed appropriate that Glass Town's chronicles were the size of the toy soldiers who inspired them. But more importantly, the tiny booklets with their tiny print were easily concealed. Even if they were discovered, it would be extremely difficult for adult eyes to decipher their hieroglyphics. From the beginning, the Brontë writing had an air of secrecy about it.

Actual Size

They had other 'plays' as well: "Our Fellows" and "The Islanders." The Islanders differed from "The Young Men" in that they were giants that were ten miles tall rather than miniature adventurers.

But at night, the plays did not end for Emily and Charlotte. Huddled together in the same bed under cover of darkness, they whispered late into the night more plays, secret plays known only to them which were so secret that they both promised never to record them. Day and night, Emily and Charlotte were perpetually creating a counter-world to that of the Parsonage.

In the summer of 1830, Patrick Brontë became ill for some months with a bronchial malady, a very Victorian concern. He always maintained that his lungs were *"delicate"* and went to great lengths to protect them — that is, great lengths of white silk — yards and yards of it wrapped in layers so thick and high that they encased the edge of his chin and brushed his earlobes. He believed that if he kept his neck and chest sufficiently warm and protected from draughts, he could keep his lungs healthy. In an age when so many succumbed to consumption, it may not have been a bad plan. When he became ill, and the illness lingered for months, he was rattled. The whole family was rattled. They had already tragically lost three members of the family. Patrick conducted at least a half dozen funerals a month at the parish church, and the Brontë front yard was a cemetery. They were never free from the specter of death, either inwardly and outwardly.

After the horror of Cowan Bridge, he had pushed the problem of his daughters' vulnerable futures aside. The thought of sending them away again was unthinkable; all the children had been safely at home for five years now. Sending Branwell away to be schooled was never a consideration. Patrick would oversee the education of his only son himself, who he believed to be undoubtedly a prodigy. But his illness brought the dilemma of his daughters back to the fore. He could no longer ignore the situation. He would start with his oldest daughter. He appealed to Charlotte's wealthy godparents about her precarious position. They kindly agreed to finance her education at an institution with which they had personal experience. Moreover, it was near their home so that they could personally keep an eye on her to ensure that all was well. When Charlotte returned, she would educate her sisters. It was all decided. In January, a terrified Charlotte tearfully embraced her family and obediently boarded a hired covered cart for her twenty mile, day long journey through the frozen Yorkshire landscape to Miss Wooler's School at Roe Head.

When she disembarked the covered cart at Roe Head, all the girls rushed to the window to get a glimpse of the new girl. What they saw confused them. Her face looked their age, but she had the clothing and countenance of a little old lady. At playtime, she not only did not know any of the games, she was completely disinterested, preferring to read books and do extra lessons.

Miss Wooler found her to be exceptionally bright with astounding reading and writing skills (she had no idea that Charlotte had been producing a monthly magazine for years), but she was nearly ignorant of arithmetic and geography. Charlotte was horrified to find herself in a class with the youngest girls. But before a month was out, she had made best friends with two other girls, Mary Taylor and Ellen Nussey, and she was the top student in the school in every subject. Charlotte blossomed at Roe Head. She discovered that she could make new friends and succeed in the world. Charlotte's departure from home, however, had a devastating effect on Glass Town and with it... a measure of intimacy with Emily that would never be regained.

With her big sister temporarily out of the picture, Emily got tired of Branwell's heavy-handed management of Glass Town. Consequently, she seceded and took Anne with her. She left everything behind, only taking with her the Palace of Instruction with its one thousand students. She and Anne emigrated to the other side of the world to an island kingdom in the North Pacific that they named Gondal. There were many significant differences in Emily's Gondal which give us a glimpse into her mind.

Gondal was a wintry landscape that shared the same climate as Yorkshire, unlike the tropical climes of Glass Town. But that was just the surface difference. Glass town was a very male dominated, militaristic place. Gondal, on the other hand, was a female dominated royalist world. Emily was inspired by the young Princess Victoria, who was her same age. In Gondal, the strong and beautiful Augusta Geraldine Almeda ruled, but not with gentleness and benevolence. She was just as ruthless as her male counterparts in Glass Town.

Gondal would, hereafter, play a major role in Emily's life. It was an addictive escape for her — Victorian style. It was very difficult and sad for all the Brontë children to eventually let go of their imaginary worlds where they had ultimate control over their own destinies and would never die. They were all well into adulthood before they finally let go, but they all did, except Emily. She would never leave Gondal, causing the deep concern of Charlotte. But Emily would continue to be emotionally fed and creatively inspired by Gondal for the rest of her life. The large majority of her poems were Gondal poems.

When Charlotte came home seven months later, she dropped her school awards and accolades at the door. All she wanted to know was the latest news from Glass Town. Emily's secession came as a complete shock. She had never supposed such a thing could happen. To her disbelief, she and Emily now dwelt on opposite ends of the world. Though their separation may have been in the world of imagination, it portended a psychological shift in Emily that had a profound effect on her relationship with Charlotte.

At this stage, however, Charlotte picked up where she left off in the adventures of Angria, a land that had been annexed to Glass Town and had now become the center of her and Branwell's imaginary adventures. After their chores were done, the Brontë children, now teenagers, eleven, thirteen, sixteen and seventeen, spent their afternoons continuing to write their plays. Though separate, they shared the news and happenings from their respective kingdoms.

Charlotte returned to school and finished Miss Wooler's program in record time. She continued to nurture her friendships with Ellen Nussey and Mary Taylor. They would become her lifelong friends. It is interesting to note that she never divulged to her closest friends her Angrian adventures though it was huge part of her life.

In 1831, Charlotte visited Ellen's home and returned the invitation a year later. Ellen's visit was an event of near cataclysmic proportion and would go down in the family history as a benchmark in time. The Brontë's had been a completely closed society. No one had ever come to stay before who was not a relative. One can only imagine the nervous preparations that attended her arrival. Ellen kept a journal of her stay at the Parsonage, and from it we have a treasure trove of descriptions of Brontë life. She described the home, their daily lives and each member of the family.

It was Emily, however, that made the strongest impression on her. At fifteen, Emily was already decidedly different. She was:

> "...the tallest person in the house except her father. Her hair, which was naturally as beautiful as Charlotte's, was in the same unbecoming frizz, and there was the same want of complexion. She had very beautiful eyes – kind, kindling, liquid eyes, but she did not often look at you; she was too reserved. Their color might be said to be dark grey, at other times dark blue, they varied so. She talked very little."

The household routine was not put on hold for Ellen. She was awakened with the rest of the family by Patrick's gunshot out the bedroom window. They ate their bland fare of porridge, boiled beef and custards and spent the evenings either sewing or reading. But the most memorable times were when the three Brontë sisters took Ellen on long rambles across the moors. Ellen noticed that Emily became a different person on the moors. It was though she became alive. She walked the moors with the joy of a prisoner who had just been set free. The moors were like an endless ocean of earth to Emily. They had the intoxicating effect on her that the sea often has on people. While on its vast expanse, she grasped her smallness, her insignificance. It put things into perspective and set her free. Charlotte wrote:

> "My sister Emily loved the moors. Flowers brighter than the rose bloomed in the blackest of the heath for her; out of a sullen hollow in the livid hill-side her mind could make an Eden. She found in the bleak solitude many and dear delight; and not the least and best loved was – liberty."

The following winter, 1834, was one of the worst in memory. Heavy grey skies oppressed the heath and its inhabitants, day after day, relentlessly battering it with biting cold, sleety rain and howling winds. The death toll in Haworth rose dramatically. Piercing through the high winds, one could often hear the low bong of:

> "funeral bells so frequently tolling and filling the air with the mournful sound – and when they were still, the 'chip chip' of the mason as he cut the grave stones in a shed close by."

Confined to the Parsonage by the severe weather, Patrick was in his study, unhappily writing more funeral sermons than ever, a task he disliked almost as much as performing marriage ceremonies. The four children, however, were happily ensconced in the warm kitchen, working on Angria and Gondal round the square table, immune to the cold and death outside.

That spring a plan was formed to launch Branwell into the world. He was the golden son upon whom all the family hopes were centered. Unlike his sisters, he had a world of opportunity open to him. The difficulty lay in which path to choose. The family believed that he was far too gifted for a career in the military or the church. He must seek his acclaim in one of the arts: literature, music or painting. He had shown considerable talent in all of them. Now he just needed some training. Patrick procured the services of Yorkshire artist William Robinson as the first step of what they all knew would be Branwell's brilliant career.

It was while he was studying under Robinson in 1835 that Branwell painted his masterpiece, not so much for his artistry, as for his subjects, his sisters. Were it not for Branwell using his sisters as models to practice his art, the world would never have known he ever held a paintbrush. Thanks to his short-lived inglorious career, he left us the only surviving likenesses of the true, though as yet unrecognized, artists in the Brontë family, Charlotte and Emily and Anne.

After several years of studying with Robinson, Branwell applied to the Royal Academy in London to become a probationary student. This was an expensive undertaking, but all the family resources would be focused on Branwell's rise to fame. Godparents once again stepped forward to help with the cost. Aunt Branwell contributed, and Charlotte would return to Roe Head as a teacher, giving a portion of her paltry earnings to Branwell's advancement.

It was also decided that Emily would go to Roe Head; her school fees would also be deducted from Charlotte's salary. Charlotte wrote, *"I am sad, very sad at the thoughts of leaving home but Duty – Necessity – these are stern mistresses who will not be disobeyed."*

Within several months of each other, Charlotte, Emily and Branwell left the Parsonage to seek their way in the world. Unlike their Angrian and Gondolian counterparts, they would all return to the Parsonage as failed adventurers.

Emily had not been away from home for ten years. She not only dreaded meeting strangers — she hated them. Now she was immersed in an environment that required her to interact with new people every day. She was terrified. Like Charlotte, she suffered huge gaps in her knowledge of arithmetic and geography and was humiliatingly placed in a class with children half her size and half her age. Charlotte was with young children as well, given the task of teaching the basics to the youngest students. Both Charlotte and Emily realized at this time that they disliked small children. This was a particularly unfortunate circumstance for two young women whose only career option was to be a teacher or governess.

Having never been children themselves, they could not understand them or relate to them on any level. They had always been treated as little adults; *"noiseless and spiritless creatures"* whose earliest memories were of religion, politics, illness and death. They found children to be silly, noisy and petty.

Emily hated school and everyone in it and made no secret of it. She refused even to look at anyone and spoke only to Charlotte. However, refusing to look at anyone or speak did not change her circumstances. Her desperation led her to discover another much more powerful weapon, she refused to eat. Increasingly thin, wan, and weak, Charlotte began to fear for Emily's very life and appealed to Miss Wooler to send Emily home. Miss Wooler readily complied. In less than three months, Emily was on her way back to the Parsonage. Anne was dispatched to Roe Head to take her place.

When Emily arrived home, she found that she was not the only one seeking sanctuary. To her surprise,

Branwell was home and telling a fantastic story of being waylaid by robbers in London. In reality, the only thing that had robbed Branwell was fear.

When Branwell set out for London, he had the world in his pocket. Along with an instilled belief in his destiny as a great artist, he carried with him the money supplied by family and friends, several letters of introduction, his portfolio and a street map of London that he had studied so thoroughly, he probably knew the city better than most locals. He spent his first night at the Chapter Coffee House, the same inn his father had frequented when he was a young man in London. When he got up the next morning, instead of going directly to the Royal Academy at Somerset House on the Thames, he decided to do a little sightseeing first.

He went to the Houses of Parliament, Westminster Abbey, St. Paul's and the Tower of London. The longer he wandered, the more overwhelmed he became. His rising anxiety all came crashing in on him when he came face to face with the masterworks of the great painters in the British Museum. He felt a huge chasm opening up between him and the masters, one that he could never hope to span. All that he ever hoped to be and all that his family thought he was now went tumbling into that dark abyss. Shattered by fear and shamed by cowardice, he wandered towards the Thames and spent hours on a bridge, staring at the water moving below him, unable to catch his reflection. He reached into his pocket, pulled out his letters of introduction, dropped them into the river and watched them float away. He spent the next week at the Castle Tavern, drowning his bitter sense of failure and insignificance. When his money was gone, he boarded a coach, without even retrieving his portfolio and returned home empty handed, telling a tall tale. He only had been gone a week.

It is interesting to note that neither Patrick nor Aunt Branwell pressed him for any more details upon his return, though they must have seen through his story. They had encountered Branwell's dark side before and did not wish to see it again. He could be charming and engaging in one moment, and in the next fly into such a rage that he could send himself into an apoplectic fit. It terrified his family, and they all took pains not to set him off.

The one place that Branwell had established himself, beyond the walls of the Parsonage, was the Black Bull Inn in Haworth village. At age eighteen, he was the only Brontë who associated with the villagers. They loved him at the Black Bull; he was clever and fun and the life of the party. One of his well known tricks was to show off his ambidexterity by writing at the same time with both hands. Some regulars even said that he could write Latin with one hand and Greek with the other at the same time. Down at the Black Bull, he was a star.

For the next three years, Emily and Branwell lived at home with their elderly father and Aunt, peaceably existing in semi-isolation. Patrick went about his rounds. Aunt stayed in her room. Branwell drank all night and slept all day. Emily busied herself with the domestic duties to which she felt very suited. The kitchen became her domain, and she took over the family baking. While her hands were busy, her mind was at work. She propped up her books to study while she kneaded the bread and peeled the potatoes, filling in those geography and grammar gaps and continuing with French and German. After chores, she worked on

Gondal and walked out on her beloved moors nearly every day in all weather. She was healthy, content and completely self-contained. She had no desire to see a new face or to have a change of routine or scenery.

She wrote a tremendous amount of poetry at this time, usually at night *"...when the moon is bright/ And the eye can wander through worlds of light."* After Aunt and Papa went to bed and Branwell left for the pub, she sat at the kitchen table and wrote by the light of her small oil lamp:

> *SILENT is the house: all are laid asleep:*
> *One alone looks out o'er the snow-wreaths deep,*
> *Watching every cloud, dreading every breeze*
> *That whirls the wildering drift,*
> *and bends the groaning trees.*
> *Cheerful is the hearth, soft the matted floor;*
> *Not one shivering gust creeps through pane or door;*
> *The little lamp burns straight;*
> *its rays shoot strong and far;*
> *I trim it well, to be the wanderer's guiding-star.*

Emily was a poet of the night. In it, she was protected from intrusions and demands. Wooed by its dark sanctuary of liberty, Emily became a lover of the night, supplicant of the moon and stars:

> *In summer's mellow midnight,*
> *A cloudless moon shone through*
> *Our open parlour window,*
> *And rose-trees wet with dew.*

I sat in silent musing;
The soft wind waved my hair;
It told me heaven was glorious,
And sleeping earth was fair.

I needed not its breathing
To bring such thoughts to me;
But still it whispered lowly,
'How dark the woods would be!

'The thick leaves in my murmur
Are rustling like a dream,
And all their myriad voices
Instinct with spirit seem.'

I said, 'Go, gentle singer,
Thy wooing voice is kind:
But do not think its music
Has power to reach my mind…

The wanderer would not heed me:
Its kiss grew warmer still:
'Oh Come!' it sighed so sweetly;
'I'll win thee 'gainst thy will.

'Were we not friends from childhood?
Have I not loved thee long?
As long as thou, the solemn night,
Whose silence wakes my song.

While Emily was blossoming in her element, Charlotte was withering at Roe Head. She was much more duty bound than Emily or Branwell. Yet, she felt that the sacrifice she was making for her family was coming to naught. The brother and sister for whom she went to work were both at home, and her salary was being garnished for Anne's tuition to learn what Charlotte could easily teach her at home. Her journal reveals her desperation:

> "Must I from day to day sit chained to this chair, prisoned within these four walls, while these glorious summer suns are burning in heaven and the year is revolving in its richest glow, and declaring at the close of each summer's day, the time I am losing will never come again."

She fell ill with the familiar symptoms. Unable to eat or sleep, she returned home for good with nervous exhaustion. Illness was once again the great rescuer for another Victorian woman.

She revived her dream of being an author and sent the current poet laureate, Robert Southey, a sample of her writing and asked his advice. While he admitted that she had a *"faculty for verse,"* he admonished her:

> "Literature cannot be the business of a woman's life, and it ought not to be. The more she is engaged in her proper duties, the less leisure will she have for it, even as an accomplishment and recreation."

He added a warning:

> "...the day dreams in which you habitually indulge are likely to induce a diseased state of mind."

He ended with the *"cooling dose"* of advice that she should keep to her sewing.

Branwell was also writing poetry, having decided that his métier was literature. He sent three letters to

Blackwood's magazine, each more pompous and desperate than the last. They were all ignored. He wrote an equally arrogant letter to William Wordsworth who also ignored the young self-important upstart.

Emily thought they were both wasting their time. For her, poetry was an ecstatic experience between her and God—a sacred communion with the divine. She did not even share her poetry with her own family, let alone an outsider. Her poem, "An Old Stoic," spells out exactly how she feels:

> *Riches I hold in light esteem*
> *And Love I laugh to scorn*
> *And Lust of Fame was but a dream*
> *That vanished with the morn--*
>
> *And if I pray--the only prayer*
> *That moves my lips for me*
> *Is--'Leave the heart that now I*
> *bear And give me liberty.'*
>
> *Yes, as my swift days near their*
> *goal 'Tis all that I implore--*
> *In life and death a chainless soul*
> *With courage to endure!*

After three years at home, Emily made an unlikely decision to take a teaching position at Law Hill, a school that was eight miles down the road from Haworth. In the 19th century, eight miles was nearly another world away. It was certainly a walkable distance but the life of a governess left little time for walking. Charlotte wrote to Ellen:

> *"I have had one letter from [Emily] since her departure, it gives an appalling account of her duties – hard labour from six in the morning until near eleven at night, with only one half-hour of exercise between. This is slavery. I fear she will never stand it."*

After a twelve hour workday of teaching and tending children, a governess was expected to spend her evenings in never ending needlework—mending, hemming, darning, and the like. She often worked until eleven at night without hope of getting to the bottom of the work pile. She did all this for fifteen to twenty pounds a year.

Beyond the physical punishment of the work was the emotional hardship of it. During a short stint as a governess, Emily wrote to Charlotte of her employer:

> *"...she cares nothing in the world about me except to contrive how the greatest possible quantity of labour may be squeezed out of me, and to that end she overwhelms me with oceans of needlework, yards of cambric to mend, muslin nightcaps to make, and, above all things, dolls to dress... I now see more clearly than I have ever done that a private governess has no existence, is not considered as a living and rational being except as connected with wearisome duties she has to fulfil."*

Governesses were treated as anonymous, faceless creatures with less worth than a workhorse, as they were more easily and cheaply replaced. As the only career open to women, governesses suffered from a high unemployment rate. There could be up to eight hundred applicants for a position that paid fifteen pounds a year. The situation for single women in England was dire.

Most likely, Emily obtained her position at Law Hill through a referral from Charlotte's employer, Miss Wooler. She was determined to try to fit herself into the outside world one more time in spite of her morbid shyness. Though her attempt could not be called a success, her term at Law Hill was a turning point in her life.

Despite hating her job and hating her students (she informed her class one morning that the house dog was dearer to her than any of them), she was still remarkably creative, writing more than a dozen poems in six months. It is not surprising that their themes were of exile, isolation, imprisonment:

> *Could I have lingered but an hour*
> *It well had paid a week of toil,*
> *But truth has banished fancy's power;*
> *I hear my dungeon bars recoil--*
>
> *Even as I stood with raptured eye,*
> *Absorbed in bliss, so deep and dear,*
> *My hour of rest had fleeted by*
> *And given me back to weary care.*

But there was a much more momentous creative work germinating in Emily's imagination than poetic laments while she was at Law Hill, one that would eventually render her name immortal. It was here that the seeds of <u>Wuthering Heights</u> were sown. Several ancient houses stood near Law Hill, each with an intriguing history of a family broken by greed and revenge. With this bit of local lore filed away in her mind, she returned to the Parsonage after six months with her health broken once more by self-induced starvation. She vowed never to leave home again.

Branwell was also back home, unanxious to leave again after a failed stint as a portrait painter in Bradford. He brought a load of debts home with him and an opium addiction. Anne also appeared back at the Parsonage when she was dismissed by the Ingham family after she, in desperation, tied her two charges to the legs of a table so that she could get on with her work.

Once home, Emily regained her health. She and Charlotte, now ages twenty and twenty-two, respectively, established a comfortable housekeeping routine in which they both flourished, having disposal of their own time. Charlotte wrote to Ellen:

> *"Emily and I are… busy as you may suppose – I manage the ironing and keep the rooms clean – Emily does the baking and attends to the kitchen – we are such odd animals that we prefer this mode of contrivance to having a new face among us…Human feelings are queer things – I am much happier black-leading the stove – making the beds and sweeping the floor at home, than I should be living like a fine lady anywhere else."*

Emily was seeing to it, however, that there were new faces among them, though not human ones. She had two pet geese, Victoria and Adelaide, named after the young Queen and her mother. She also had a merlin hawk named Hero that she had nursed and tamed after finding him wounded on the moors. And there was also

Black Tom, Anne's cat, and a great bull-mastiff dog named Keeper.

Keeper was a devil of a dog that intimidated everyone but Emily. One of the few occasions when the villagers saw the parson's mysterious daughter was when Keeper got into a fight with another village dog. Emily flew out of the house with a tin of pepper, extricated the snarling dog from the fight with her bare hands holding him *"round the neck with one arm, while with the other hand she dredge[d] their noses with pepper."* Then she drove the simpering animal into the house, leaving the onlookers *"thunderstruck at the deed."*

When it came to animals, Emily was entirely comfortable, contrary to the deer-like skittishness she displayed around people. Even when the postman or the butcher came to the door of the Parsonage, she scampered into the kitchen. Yet, when she was bitten by a rabid dog she was utterly unflappable. She dispassionately examined the wound and, without a word, marched into the house, picked up a hot iron and laid it on her arm to cauterize the gash.

While accumulating her menagerie and busying herself with domestic chores, Emily was writing prolifically. She carried pencil and paper in her apron pockets so that she could stop whatever she was doing to jot down her thoughts as they came to her. At night, she would work the fragments into poems or into the Gondal narrative. She lived for these hours of solitude when she could focus on her most fulfilling work, poetry. As she embraced poetry as her vocation, she became more remote even to her family. Her siblings were trying to find their footing outside the Parsonage.

Anne secured another governess position with a family named Robinson. Branwell found a job as a tutor, but after being dismissed for drunkenness became a railway clerk. Both jobs paid more than four times as much as a governess and required far fewer hours. This latest development further dampened Charlotte's affection for her brother. She was finding it increasingly difficult to hide her disappointment in his long fall from brilliant artist to railway clerk. It angered her that her brother, who had all the opportunities open to him that were closed to her, was squandering his life in dissipation.

Abhorred by the thought of being enslaved again by demanding employers, Charlotte *"hatched"* a plan to establish their own school, The Miss Brontës' Establishment. Of course, Emily disliked the idea, as it would seriously curtail her privacy and freedom. But she could not refuse, as it would offer freedom for Charlotte and Anne. They proposed the idea to Papa and Aunt and found them both not only agreeable, but Aunt was willing to provide necessary funding.

While they were still in the planning stages, Charlotte received a letter from her friend, Mary Taylor's sister Martha, who was attending a fashionable young ladies school in Brussels. Martha wrote vivid descriptions of Brussels' museums and cathedrals and urged her to come to Brussels for more education so that she could attract more wealthy students to her school. Martha's letter captured Charlotte's imagination and for the first time, she was fired with *"a strong wish for wings...such a thirst to see – to know – to learn – something internal seemed to expand boldly..."* The woman who had never been more than fifty miles from home had awakened to the world beyond the Parsonage doors.

There was much to do to turn this new dream into a reality. First, she had to convince Aunt Bran to fund their education rather than to found a school, and she had to find a school in Brussels that they could reasonably afford. Most difficult of all, she had to persuade Emily to go. It took more than a year, but when she had accomplished all these things, Patrick, who was sixty-four years old and had never been abroad, decided to escort his daughters across the channel.

The fourteen hour crossing was not a smooth one. Charlotte spent it in her cabin miserably seasick. However, Emily stayed on deck, drawn to the untamed sea as she was to the raw, rugged moors of Yorkshire. She was transfixed by the dark tumultuous waves, undisturbed by wind and sea spray. But from the moment she stepped off the boat in Belgium, she was miserable.

As they traveled by coach across the countryside, they saw that every bit of land was tilled and cultivated. There were no open, empty spaces, nothing untouched by man. Emily felt hemmed in. Her sense of entrapment grew with their arrival in Brussels. They made their way through the winding, twisting streets until they found their new school, the Heger Pensionnat, on the narrow Rue d'Isabelle, one indistinguishable door in a long row of identical doors and windows in the shadow of more endless rows of doors and windows. She felt like a mouse in a maze with no way out.

The Heger Pensionnat was quite pleasant and airy and opened up at the back to a beautiful hidden garden. Charlotte was enchanted with everything. This was the promised land for her. But one small patch of landscaped earth enclosed on all sides by labyrinthine walls and masses of humanity left Emily feeling desperately caged.

The Brontë sisters were an odd looking pair in their dark old fashioned frocks. They appeared in the Pensionnat as though they had been plucked from another place and time. Emily, in particular, was still wearing puffy leg 'o mutton sleeves, which had been out of fashion for nearly twenty years. Her tall, angular five foot seven frame, *"lean and scant,"* was accentuated by her refusal to wear cumbersome petticoats beneath her skirt. She towered over her sister, who was less than five feet tall, by her own description, *"stunted...broad and dumpy."* The two, by Branwell's description, were:

> *"Distant and distrait, large of nose, small of figure, red of hair, prominent of spectacles* (speaking of Charlotte), *showing great intellectual development, but eyes constantly cast down, very silently, painfully retiring."*

Emily built an inner fortress to protect herself from the fortress Pensionnat, and she hurled fiery arrows at anyone who tried to penetrate it. Being distant and withdrawn was not self-protective enough. She was hostile, like a wounded animal, to everyone and everything at the Pensionnat. Furthermore, she kept her sister in isolation with her.

She literally leaned on Charlotte, as though weak and unable to stand on her own, a strange posture for the taller and stronger of the two of them. During classes, she insisted that she and Charlotte sit in the last row of desks in the furthest corner away from the rest of the pupils. She refused to speak to anyone and did not want Charlotte to speak to anyone either. She partitioned their beds at the end of the dormitory from the others with a white curtain. Her fear and unhappiness came across as arrogance and rudeness.

Her relationship with her teacher, M. Heger, was adversarial from the start. She feared that if she accepted his instruction she would *"lose all originality of thought and expression."* In time, M. Heger realized that he was not merely dealing with a shy or rebellious student, but that he had a mind of uncommon strength and originality on his hands. He found her to be *"egotistical and exacting"* but with:

> *"...a head for logic and a capability of argument unusual in a man and rare indeed in a woman...[but] impairing this gift was her stubborn tenacity of will which rendered her obtuse to all reasoning where her own wishes, or her own sense of right was concerned."*

In Heger's view, Emily's ego, logic and tenacity rendered her difficult and obtuse; whereas, had she been a man, her gifts would have been considered useful. He mused:

> *"She should have been a man – a great navigator. Her powerful reason would have deduced new spheres of discovery from the knowledge of the old; and her strong imperious will would never have been daunted by opposition or difficulty..."*

He also remarked on the *"tyranny"* with which she bound her sister. It was obvious that Charlotte wanted to be there and a part of the life of the Pensionnat. But she was torn between her own desires and the need to keep Emily from imploding. After all, it was she who had brought her there. Even she could not fail to see that Emily's shyness converted to hostility was now verging on mental illness. Though it may not have seemed so, Emily was trying for Charlotte's sake, but her inner battles were wearing her down. Her mental state soon translated to physical illness. She lost the will to eat and became too distraught to sleep. *"...the same suffering and conflict ensued..."* wrote Charlotte of Emily's tenure on the continent:

> "Once more she seemed sinking... She did conquer: but the victory cost her dear. She was never happy till she [was] back to the remote English village, the old Parsonage house, and desolate Yorkshire Hills."

It was not illness this time that bore Emily home; it was death. On a drear November day, Charlotte and Emily received the black bordered envelope by post giving them the news that Aunt Bran had died of an intestinal obstruction. They packed their boxes and sailed home ten months after their arrival in Belgium.

When they arrived home, they found a house in disarray in Aunt's absence and inhabited by two helpless men, their father and Branwell, who were mystified when dinner did not show up on a tray at their rooms on the hour or why dust was gathering on the piano. Order was not the only thing missing from the Parsonage; Victoria, Adelaide and Hero were gone, handily dispensed of by Aunt Bran before she died. They had expected to see the animals, but they had not expected to see Branwell at home.

Branwell had been home for nine months with never a word said about it by letter from Aunt Bran or Patrick.

He had left his railway clerk position in disgrace. The till had been robbed while he was at the local pub, and the account books were filled with poetry and drawings rather than tidy sums and differences. Charlotte's affection for her brother was at an end. She was disgusted. He may as well have been called Bran-ne'er-do-well, as far as she was concerned. On the other hand, Emily tended to Branwell as though he were one of her wounded creatures from the moor.

Aunt Bran had drawn up her will nine years before she died while Branwell's prospects were still golden. Assuming that her favored nephew would be self-sufficient, she left everything to her nieces. Emily, Charlotte, and Anne each received a legacy of three hundred fifty pounds. After close and protracted study of the newspapers, Emily advised that they invest their money in that new technology: the railroad. With their newfound wealth, Emily turned inward while Charlotte turned outward.

Charlotte went back to Belgium to resume her studies and experience in Brussels, unencumbered by her unwilling sister. Emily was now mistress of the Parsonage and free to order her life as she wished. She flourished in her freedom and it showed. She was not only free to write and to roam her beloved moors at will, but she was free to eat at will. She called Tabby back (who had also been dispensed of by Aunt Bran), and the two of them kept a comfortable house and a warm kitchen where Emily became *"solid...as a dumpling."* Emily wrote:

> *"I'll walk where my own nature would be leading;*
> *It vexes me to choose another guide."*

Emily, at age twenty-four, was wholly disconnected from the need for outside stimulation and praise. She not only distrusted it, she felt violated and intruded upon by it. Her core need was the freedom to follow her inner lights for a sense of wholeness and wellbeing. Self-sufficiency in solitude was her sacred practice. As she retreated from the construct of human society, she immersed herself further into the construction of her imaginary childhood world of Gondal. Much of her poetry was generated there. She greatly preferred her own society to any the world could offer:

> *Where pleasure still will lead to wrong,*
> *And helpless Reason warn in vain*
> *And truth is weak and Treachery strong*
> *And joy the shortest path to Pain.*
>
> *And Peace the lethargy of grief*
> *And Hope, a phantom of the soul;*
> *And Life a labour void and brief*
> *And death, the despot of the whole!*

Emily's nature was leading her to walk within. She was the great navigator that M. Heger saw in her, but she was navigating a territory far more vast than the seven seas. She was venturing into the interior of the mind, a journey that few intrepid souls ever take. We christen these spiritual sojourners mystics, prophets and poets. Their willingness to journey into unseen realms is what separates them from the rest of us, who fear our aloneness and what we might find there. But for Emily, her interior was the only place that would not disappoint. Unlike the outer world, she had control in her inner world. She was safe from loss and pain and betrayal.

To Imagination

When weary with the long day's care,
* And earthly change from pain to pain,*
And lost, and ready to despair,
* Thy kind voice calls me back again:*
Oh, my true friend! I am not lone,
While then canst speak with such a tone!

So hopeless is the world without;
* The world within I doubly prize;*
Thy world, where guile, and hate, and doubt,
* And cold suspicion never rise;*
Where thou, and I, and Liberty,
Have undisputed sovereignty.

What matters it, that all around
* Danger, and guilt, and darkness lie,*
If but within our bosom's bound
* We hold a bright, untroubled sky,*
Warm with ten thousand mingled rays
Of suns that know no winter days?

Reason, indeed, may oft complain
* For Nature's sad reality.*
And tell the suffering heart how vain
* Its cherished dreams must always be;*
And Truth may rudely trample down'
The flowers of Fancy, newly-blown:

But thou art ever there, to bring
* The hovering vision back, and breathe*
New glories o'er the blighted spring,
* And call a lovelier Life from Death.*
And whisper, with a voice divine,
Of real world, as bright as thine.

Emily Brontë

I trust not to thy phantom bliss,
    Yet, still, in evening's quiet hour,
With never-failing thankfulness,
    I welcome thee, Benignant Power;
Sure solacer of human cares,
And sweeter hope, when hope despairs!

At this point, Emily was in full retreat, vowing to never leave home again. She happily busied herself with household chores. Unlike many other women who feel housework to be enslavement, Emily found it liberating. The mechanics of housework freed her mind to mentally flourish. She conjugated German verbs and mentally translated English poems she knew by heart into French while she kneaded the bread dough, ironed the sheets and swept the flagstone entrance hall. By day, she achieved the perfect marriage of two planes, domestic and intellectual. By night, she became the metaphysical poet of the moors:

I gazed upon the cloudless moon
And loved her all the night
'Til morning came and ardent noon,
Then I forgot her light –

No – not forgot, eternally
Remains its memory dear; But
could the day seem dark to me
Because the night was fair?

At this time, Patrick's eyesight had begun to seriously deteriorate. He became increasingly dependent upon Emily, his only child living at home. Though his pride as well as his vision suffered, father and daughter developed a strong bond. Despite failing eyesight, Patrick was still fond of his pistols, and continued to start each morning by firing at his own church tower. The nearly blind old man decided to teach Emily how to shoot.

Her shooting lessons were observed and recorded by John Greenwood, the village stationer. Because he supplied the Brontës' with writing supplies, he was one of the few villagers who had contact with them. He was obviously fascinated by the reclusive family on the hill. His account, though idealized, gives an interesting window into an afternoon at the Parsonage in 1843:

> *"'Now my dear girl, let me see how well you can shoot today'. 'Yes Papa' and away she would run to the bottom of the garden, putting (the board) in proper position, then returning... take the pistol which he had previously primed and loaded for her. 'Now my girl, he would say, 'take time, be steady.' 'yes Papa' she would say taking the weapon with as firm a hand and as steady an eye as any veteran of the camp and fire. Then she would run to fetch the board for him to see how she had succeeded. And she did get so proficient that she was rarely far from the mark. 'How cleverly you have done, my dear girl'... she would return to him the pistol, saying 'Load again Papa' and away she would go to the kitchen, roll another shelf-full of tea cakes, then wiping her hands, she would return again to the garden and call out 'I'm ready again Papa' and so they would go on until he thought she had had enough practice for the day. "Oh, he would exclaim, she is a brave and noble girl. She is my right hand."*

On New Year's Day 1844, Charlotte returned home from Brussels in dejection. Her venture into the world had been aborted by her forbidden love for her teacher, M. Heger, who was a married man. She was escorted by her would-be paramour's wife to the dock and shipped back home in lovesick disgrace. Upon her return home, she was tortured not only by her unrequited feelings for Heger, but by a new distance between Emily and herself.

Emily, who had until this time been the younger submissive sister, had come into her own at home; whereas, Charlotte felt alone, adrift and isolated. For the first time in their lives while living under the same roof, Charlotte and Emily slept apart. While Charlotte assumed Aunt Bran's empty bedroom with the fireplace, sleeping in the same bed where her mother, sisters and aunt had died, Emily remained on her cot in the spare unheated children's study, her hermit's cell.

With her education completed, Charlotte again took up the dream of establishing a small school for girls at the Parsonage. She was frustrated by Emily's refusal to help with the school beyond fixing meals for the students. She was not about to give up her mind again to any other occupation but her own mental pursuits.

In fact, Emily was devoting herself more than ever to her writing. In February 1844, she sat down and inventoried all her poems to date—destroying some, revising others and writing new ones. She was at the peak of her poetry production. She organized her poems into two booklets. One she called "Gondal Poems," and the other she titled simply "E.J.B. Transcribed February 1844." Though one set of poems was derived from her fantasy world and the other from her real life, they all shared the same themes: rebellion, isolation, estrangement and liberation. Like Emily

Dickinson, Emily Brontë's writing was an intimate experience of private ecstasy that she shared with no one — both poets would not even share with their sisters.

Unlike Emily, Charlotte felt stifled and suffocated at home. She felt *"buried"* by the monotony of changeless days. She wrote to Ellen:

> *"I can hardly tell you how time gets on... at Haworth – There is no event whatever to mark its progress – one day resembles another...Life wears away – I shall soon be 30 – and I have done nothing yet."*

But change came with the warmer months. May brought a new face to the Parsonage. A twenty-nine year old Irish curate named Arthur Bell Nicholls came to assist Patrick, who was now virtually blind, with his pastoral duties. Emily and Charlotte regarded him as an uninteresting necessity to the household and kept a cold distance from him.

More interesting was Anne's return in June from Thorp Green after four years as a governess for the Robinson family. When she arrived, she was more than tired. She seemed shaken by something she did not want to discuss. The source of her agitation was revealed when Branwell returned on July 17 from the Robinson family with a threatening dismissal letter from his employer.

The fact that neither Anne nor Mr. Robinson specified the reason for Branwell's dismissal leads one to believe that the offense was too horrible to name. However, Branwell repeated his version of the story to anyone who would listen. According to him, for several years he had been engaged in an adulterous affair with Mrs. Robinson, the forty-three year old mother of his young pupil. He was dismissed when Mr. Robinson found them out.

Neither his father nor his sisters questioned his story or pressed him for details—just as they had not when he returned home from London with a tall story about being robbed. Anne remained silent on the matter. She seemed unwilling to name Branwell's indiscretion even to herself in her private diary, only going so far as to refer to an *"undreamt-of experience of human nature"* that she had the misfortune to witness at Thorp Green. Whatever happened at the Robinson's proved to be Branwell's final undoing. He lost all self-control and spiraled into a dark abyss from which only death would eventually release him.

Charlotte wrote to Ellen that Branwell *"thought of nothing but stunning and drowning his distress of mind"* with laudanum and drink. His life was a misery. In fact, he wailed that he was literally haunted by a woman shrouded in black who called herself *'MISERY'* who *"walked by my side and leant on my arm as affectionately as if she were my legal wife."*

He made sure that the entire household shared his misery. He effectively held the family hostage with his drunken rages, badgering them for money for his drugs and alcohol and running up debts all over town. He even set his bed on fire by knocking over a candle while he was passed out. Charlotte wrote:

> *"So long as he remains at home, I scarce dare hope for peace in the house. We must all, I fear, prepare for a season of distress and disquietude."*

Branwell's antics broke up the tedium of days, but this was not the break for which Charlotte had hoped. With her drunken brother wreaking havoc in the house, she had to abandon all plans for her school. Her father was blind, her brother was dissipated, the dream of her school was gone, her love interest could never be consummated and her relationship with Emily was strained. She felt utterly powerless and without hope. Charlotte fell into a deep depression that was only broken by the rage that she felt towards Branwell, who had squandered every opportunity that she had been denied.

Anne was suffering her own malaise, *"I for my part cannot well be flatter or older in mind than I am now."*

Emily seemed to be the only Brontë untouched by the dark despondency of the Parsonage, which is a testament to how thoroughly she had built her inner strength. She existed in sublime isolation even from her family. In her diary she wrote:

> *"I am quite contented for myself…altogether as hearty and having learnt to make the most of the present…and merely desiring that everybody should be as comfortable as myself and undesponding, and then we should have a very tolerable world of it. "*

Unruffled by the grief of those around her, she continued to move through her days of household duties mingled with her personal studies. By night she continued to invent her verses while she waited up to open the door for Branwell at whatever hour he came in from the Black Bull Tavern and haul him up the stairs to his bed. She cared for her tortured, inebriated brother the same way she nursed the wounded animals she found on the moors. Were it not for one singular event on an autumn day in October 1845, Emily's prized solitude would have continued uninterrupted. Charlotte's sense of entombment would have continued unabated. They both would have died in obscurity, and the world would have been poorer for it.

Emily absentmindedly left her rosewood lap desk open in the parlor. As Charlotte scurried about, perhaps muttering epithets against her untidy sister whose messes she had to straighten up too often, she found two dark crimson, leather bound manuscript books containing Emily's poems. Undoubtedly, she struggled against the inner conflict of invading her sister's obsessively guarded privacy, knowing that:

> "Emily was not a person of demonstrative character, nor one on the recesses of whose mind and feelings even those nearest and dearest to her could, with impunity, intrude unlicensed."

But Charlotte could not resist the lines she found in her sister's handwriting. Emily's *"[un]common effusions... vigorous and genuine"* drew her in like a magnet from which she could not pull away:

> "They stirred my heart like the sound of a trumpet... To my ear, they had... a peculiar music – wild, melancholy, and elevating."

Spellbound and enthralled, she anxiously flipped page after page, even scribbling beneath one poem:

> "Never was better stuff penned."

Emily's poems relit a fire within Charlotte that had been snuffed out years before-- publication. But first, she had to confess to Emily her violation:

> *"It took hours to reconcile her to the discovery I had made, and days to persuade her that such poems merited publication. I knew, however, that a mind like hers could not be without honourable ambition, and refused to be discouraged in my attempts to fan that spark to flame."*

Anne joined the effort to persuade Emily to publish by bringing out her own verses, asking Charlotte if she *"might like to look at hers too."*

Charlotte's discovery of Emily's poetry changed their lives and the literary world forever. After being cloistered at the Parsonage for two years, Charlotte finally saw a way out: authorship. Emily reluctantly agreed to publication on the condition of anonymity. A new era for the Brontë sisters was beginning.

For the first time in ten years, after the day's work was done and Papa was asleep and Branwell was well on his way to inebriation at the Black Bull, the sisters gathered around the kitchen table by lamplight to read, to discuss rhyme, meter and metaphor and to write. It was during these sessions that Emily wrote her finest poem, "No Coward Soul is Mine" which reaffirmed her repudiation of organized religion and worldly ambition and her attachment to the Infinity within her own soul which vanquished even Death:

Emily Brontë

No coward soul is mine,
No trembler in the world's storm-troubled sphere:
I see Heaven's glories shine,
And faith shines equal, arming me from fear.

O God within my breast,
Almighty, ever-present Deity!
Life--that in me has rest,
As I--undying Life--have power in thee!

Vain are the thousand creeds
That move men's hearts: unutterably vain;
Worthless as withered weeds,
Or idlest froth amid the boundless main,

To waken doubt in one
Holding so fast by thine infinity;
So surely anchored on
The stedfast rock of immortality.

With wide-embracing love
Thy spirit animates eternal years,
Pervades and broods above,
Changes, sustains, dissolves, creates, and rears.

Though earth and man were gone,
And suns and universes ceased to be,
And Thou were left alone,
Every existence would exist in Thee.

There is not room for Death,
Nor atom that his might could render void:
Thou--THOU art Being and Breath,
And what THOU art may never be destroyed.

This is the penultimate surviving poem that came from Emily's pen. Its expression resonates more closely with the novel she would soon embark upon, *Wuthering Heights*, than with the two hundred poems that she had been writing since 1836. In fact, it seems to span the space between Emily the poet and Emily the novelist.

After many late nights of creation and collaboration, Emily and Anne each chose twenty-one poems and Charlotte chose nineteen for inclusion in their little volume of poetry. They settled on pseudonyms that would disguise their gender and correspond with their initials — Currer (Charlotte), Ellis (Emily), and Acton (Anne) Bell. The surname they lifted from their father's curate, Arthur Bell Nicholls. Charlotte commenced her search for a publisher. After several rejections, she finally found a bookseller who consented to publish their poems at the authors' expense. This they consented to do and spent a portion of their small inheritance from Aunt Bran to finance the publication.

Before their book of poetry saw the light of day, they immediately launched into the writing of their novels. Well aware that a career in writing was their last hope for an independent income, they recognized that the novel, a relatively new art form, was a more *"saleable article"* with a larger audience than poetry. Perhaps they got the idea from Branwell, who had already begun a novel that he worked on spurtively during his more lucid moments. He called his novel *And The Weary Are At Rest.* The title seems to be a wish fulfillment for his own anguished life. The story also paralleled his life of adultery and heartbreak. Unlike his sisters who wrote secretly and consistently, Branwell bragged about his novel, saying that he could write a bestseller while *"smoking a cigar and...humming a tune."* He was sure that this was the creative endeavor that would finally bring him the recognition he deserved. Unfortunately, he also did not have the work ethic that his sisters had. It took more than smoking cigars and humming tunes to write a book. He never finished the project.

Charlotte and Anne's novels also fall along the lines of personal wish fulfillments, seeking to redress past wrongs and create the futures of their choosing. Anne's main character, Agnes Grey, is rescued from her soul-destroying life of servitude as a governess by the man of her dreams, Edward Weston. Charlotte did little to disguise the inspiration for her novel, <u>The Professor</u>. Set in Brussels, the site of her former school, its main character, the professor of the title, is directly modeled after her erstwhile failed love interest, M. Heger. However, the professor of Charlotte's creation actually falls in love with a timorous governess and rescues her from a life of insignificance. Together, they escape from an evil headmistress named Zoraide, obviously modeled on M. Heger's wife.

However, there is no happy ending in Emily's novel, <u>Wuthering Heights</u>—though it does not mean that it is not also autobiographical or a wish fulfillment. It is the tale of two lovers, Catherine and Heathcliff, who seem to be human embodiments of the elemental forces of the Yorkshire moors where the story is set. Their wild and untamed passion is as rugged and unforgiving as the wind and rain that incessantly beats on the northern heathered hills. To subdue or control it would be as impossible as commanding the storms to cease. When Nelly questions Catherine's attachment to Heathcliff, Catherine tries to explain, in human language inadequate to express such spiritual union:

> "...he is more myself than I am. Whatever our souls are made of, his and mine are the same... If all else perished, and he remained, I should still continue to be; and if all else remained, and he were annihilated, the universe would turn to a mighty stranger. I should not seem a part of it... Nelly, I **am** Heathcliff— he's always in my mind — not as a pleasure-- but as my own being..."

In the end, their passion claims them, and their love finally finds consummation beyond earthly bounds.

Catherine and Heathcliff capture Emily's supernatural connection with the natural world and her struggle to experience and express her infinite inner passion within a finite world. The lines between human feeling and feral rapture are blurred. Their relationship to each other and to their world is unresolvable, therefore, destructive. They can only be reconciled when immortal is released from mortal — their spiritual union superseding their physical union.

By the time the sisters finished their novels, they had been turned down for publication by the publishers of their poetry. Despite several favorable reviews, particularly for Ellis Bell whose poetry had *"an evident power of wing,"* only two volumes of their poetry had been sold. Adding to their disappointment was the increasing pressure of caring for their aging father and raging brother. Patrick's progressive descent into blindness caused him to become increasingly dependent and cranky. He was unable to continue to help manage Branwell, whose violent outrages were becoming more dangerous.

The Parsonage had become a hellhole of hysteria when a representative of Branwell's former employer delivered the news that Mr. Robinson had died with a stipulation in his will that his widow was to be disinherited if she ever had contact with Branwell again.

Branwell received the news by going into a fit, *"bleating like a calf."* He held a gun to his head threatening to blow his brains out. He brandished a carving knife, threatening to slit his throat. He lashed out, wildly slashing through the air at anyone who tried to reason with him, bellowing that either he or they *"would be dead by morning."* Charlotte wrote:

> *"...the death of Mr. Robinson... served Branwell for a pretext to throw all about him into hubbub and confusion with his emotion... he then became intolerable. To Papa he allows rest neither day nor night, and he is continually screwing money out of him, sometimes threatening that he will kill himself if it is withheld from him."*

Even Emily, who had shown more compassion and reserved judgment for Branwell than anyone, had finally conceded that he was *"a hopeless being – it is too true."* Charlotte said, *"In his present state it is scarcely possible to stay in the room where he is."*

There was nothing to be done for Branwell, but there was hope for Papa's eyesight. Charlotte, ever being the protective daughter who was willing to interact with the world, traveled with Patrick to Manchester to consult with an eye doctor about her father's condition. There, Dr. Wilson assured them that an operation to remove Patrick's cataracts would improve his vision. The operation, performed without anesthetic, would take fifteen minutes. A month long stay for recuperation would also be required.

At Patrick's request, Charlotte was present during the surgery and was deeply moved by *"his extraordinary patience and firmness"* during the ordeal. As they settled in for Patrick's month long recuperation, Charlotte worried how her sisters would manage on their own at home with their dissolute brother, *"they too will have their troubles."*

However, as she waited in quiet darkness while attending her father, Charlotte took advantage of the solitude to draw up a list of publishers to whom they could send their manuscripts. She began her second novel. By the time she and her newly sighted father returned to Haworth a month later, <u>Jane Eyre</u> was well underway and her tenacious shopping for a publisher commenced.

Charlotte placed all three manuscripts in brown paper wrapping and began sending the package to each publisher on her list, one at a time. Each time the package was returned, she simply crossed out the name and address of the returning publisher, wrote the next name on the list and sent the package back out. This meant that each time a new publisher received the manuscripts he could see where the manuscripts had been and who had rejected them to date.

While their manuscripts made the rounds of publishers, all three sisters worked on their second novels during the coldest winter in memory. Charlotte wrote to Ellen in December 1864:

> *"The sky looks like ice. The earth is frozen, the wind is as keen as a two-edged blade. I cannot keep myself warm."*

They were all ill with colds. Charlotte was plagued with her old foes, toothaches and sleeplessness. Patrick struggled with his old enemy, depression. Charlotte related the details to Ellen with acerbic humor:

> *"...we are all in the full enjoyment of colds; much blowing of noses is heard, and much making of gruel goes on in the house."*

Charlotte, Emily and Anne sustained themselves during the dark days and lingering illness of winter around the kitchen table writing, sharing and critiquing their second novels. It was a sisterhood of creative community that was so exclusive and so clandestine that neither Patrick nor Branwell were aware of their activities. In the many missives that Charlotte wrote to her best friend, Ellen Nussey, she never once mentioned their work.

Finally, in July 1865, London publisher Thomas Cautley Newby wrote to say that he would be pleased to accept *Wuthering Heights* and *Agnes Grey* for publication. However, he rejected *The Professor*. His terms were little better than what Aylott and James offered for their poems. But Emily and Anne accepted them. Charlotte put *The Professor* in a new brown wrapper and sent it to the next publisher on her list, Smith, Elder & Co.

One month later Smith, Elder sent word to Charlotte that they also declined to publish *The Professor*. They were impressed enough with her work, however, that if she had another manuscript to send them, they would be happy to consider it. Charlotte had *Jane Eyre* in William Smith William's hands before the month was over. He read it immediately and passed it on to the firm's director, George Smith.

George Smith began reading *Jane Eyre* on a Sunday morning. He was so engrossed by it that he cancelled a noon appointment to continue reading, and he took dinner on a tray in his study that evening. He finished the book before he went to bed. The next morning, he wrote Charlotte a glowing letter of acceptance that reached her in less than a week after she sent the manuscript.

In the month of September, all three sisters received proofs from their publishers which they carefully corrected and returned. Newby proceeded to allow *Wuthering Heights* and *Agnes Grey* to carelessly slip to the bottom of the pile; whereas, Smith, Elder released *Jane Eyre* to the public on October 16. It was an immediate sensation. Bookshops sold out so quickly that the book went into its second printing almost immediately. The waiting list for the book was so long at the library readers had to wait months for it. William Makepeace Thackeray wrote to George Smith that he *"lost (or won if you like) a whole day in it at the busiest period..."*

The fact that Smith, Elder had a bestseller with *Jane Eyre* was not lost on the unscrupulous Newby. In his haste to capitalize on London's *Jane Eyre* fever, he rushed *Wuthering Heights* and *Agnes Grey* to print using the uncorrected proofs, pressuring the typesetters to hurriedly set the print without taking time to make corrections. The finished products *"abound[ed] with errors...to a mortifying degree."* Furthermore, Newby deliberately confused the names of Ellis and Acton Bell with Currer, hoping that the reading public would think the same person authored all three books, thus ensuring large sales.

The Bells' novels were reviewed in all the London papers and magazines. The reviews for *Jane Eyre* were highly positive. "The Era" pronounced that *"for power of thought and expression we do not know its rival among modern productions."* However, *Wuthering Heights* was reviewed with a bewildered mixture of *"awe and censure."* "Douglas Jerrold's Weekly Magazine" did not know what to make of it:

> *"There seems to be a great power in the book, but it is a purposeless power... the reader is shocked, disgusted, almost sickened by details of cruelty, inhumanity and the most diabolical hate and vengeance and anon come passages of powerful testimony to the supreme power of love."*

The "Atlas" observed:

> *"There are evidences in every chapter of a sort of rugged power – an unconscious strength... a more natural, unnatural story we do not remember."*

One reviewer surmised the novel with an anecdote:

> *"There is an old saying that those who eat toasted cheese at night will dream of Lucifer. The author of Wuthering Heights had evidently eaten toasted cheese."*

Readers everywhere were drawn to the story on an organic, soulful level but they were conflicted about their attraction to its *"wild, confused brutality and cruel, semi-savage love and unnatural horrors."* The common thread throughout all the reviews is that of *"power."* The honest, emotional force underlying the stories stirred the soul to the point of discomfiture, particularly because they are told from the point of view of women. How could a man write such women? Yet, how could women write with such strength and power? Moreover, how dare they write with such strength and power?

The gender of the authors was an even hotter topic in London than the novels themselves. A man writing with such power was admirable, but a woman writing thus was not only unacceptable, it was *"coarse, brutal, depraved and vulgar."* Reviewers clamored for an interview with the unknown Currer and Ellis Bell. But the mysterious authors were nowhere to be found.

In fact, the 'Bell brothers' were cloistered in their Yorkshire hermitage preparing for another onslaught of winter. Currer was ironing the bed sheets; Ellis was baking bread; Acton was rocking in her chair near the fire with her sewing in her lap. Father was locked away in his study with his books and sermons. Branwell was drowning his sorrows in drink. Neither of them was aware that there were three bestselling novelists in the house. As for the novelists, they continued their usual correspondence with friends, noting there was very little to tell really, except that the east wind had returned bringing with it the usual coughs and colds, *"a very uninteresting wind."*

It took two months for *Jane Eyre* to reach Haworth. Charlotte had seen a clergyman reading it who recognized Lowood as Cowan Bridge School and Mr. Brocklehurst as William Carus Wilson. Their secret was out. Maintaining their façade of serene anonymity would be impossible now that fame and money was at their threshold. The sisters decided to tell their father about their books. Charlotte was first. She knocked on the door to Patrick's study with her book in hand along with some reviews and announced:

> "Papa, I've been writing a book."
> "Have you, my dear?'
> "Yes, and I want you to read it."
> "I'm afraid it will try my eyes too much."
> "But it is not in manuscript; it is printed."
> "My dear! You've never thought of the expense it will be! It will almost sure to be a loss; for how can you get a book sold? No one knows you or your name."
> "But, Papa, I don't think it will be a loss…"

She sat down and read him some reviews, gave him a copy of _Jane Eyre_ and left him to read it. When he came to dinner that evening he said, "Girls, do you know Charlotte has been writing a book, and it is much better than likely?" When he finished, Emily and Anne gave him their books as well. Interestingly, they still kept their writing a secret from Branwell and their good friend, Ellen.

In the meantime, Charlotte reluctantly refused several invitations from George Smith to come to London to visit the literary world in which her book had become such a rage. However, Emily stridently vetoed any such action, holding Charlotte to her promise that they would publish only on condition of anonymity.

The following July, Newby published Anne's _The Tenant of Wildfell Hall_, again deliberately falsely advertising it as another novel by the best selling Currer Bell.

Newby's perfidy brought Charlotte's integrity and contract into question with Smith, Elder. When George Smith wrote her an inquiry on the matter, she felt bound to go to London to clear up the situation. After heated exchanges with Emily and an uncomfortably silent dinner, Charlotte and Anne were on the train for London after promising to divulge only their own identities.

When Charlotte and Anne found their way to the publishing house of Smith, Elder at 65 Cornhill and confessed to being the authors of *Jane Eyre* and *Agnes Grey*, George Smith could hardly believe that these *two rather quaintly dressed little ladies, pale-faced and anxious-looking* penned the powerful books that were causing such ferment in London:

> "They were like curious but very timid animals plucked out of their natural environment and set down in an alien one which both dazzled and frightened them."

Though he swallowed his astonishment as quickly as possible, Charlotte read the look on his face immediately. He *"must have thought us queer, quizzical-looking beings, especially me with my spectacles."*

Smith immediately made plans to squire the two celebrated authors around London, inviting them to the opera and to dinner with Thackeray and Charles Dickens. But Charlotte and Anne declined, saying that they had come to London only to see him and Mr. Newby. They preferred to remain anonymous to the rest of London. Charlotte wrote to her friend, Mary Taylor, that she *"paid for the excitement of the interview by a thundering headache and harassing sickness."* However,

Anne was *"calm and gentle, as she always is."* Perhaps part of the cause of Charlotte's headache was the fact that she had *"committed a grand error in betraying [Emily's] identity"* when she let slip *"we are three sisters"* in the course of conversation with George Smith.

Emily's wrath, however, did not deter Charlotte's focus from promoting their careers as writers. She arranged with Smith, Elder to re-issue their book of poetry, which would surely sell now that their names were well known. And Anne's second novel <u>The Tenant of Wildfell Hall</u> was receiving great acclaim.

The Brontë sisters were reaching the peak of their literary careers. They had found fame and fortune overnight that they could have hardly imagined. But just as swiftly as their literary stars had risen, tragedy was about to plummet the Brontë's into calamity of cataclysmic proportions. It was nothing less than a family holocaust.

It began with Branwell whose condition was deteriorating. He no longer blamed Mrs. Robinson for his downfall. Now he blamed the devil. He lamented, *"I shall never be able to realize the sanguine hopes of my friends, for…I am a thoroughly **old man** – mentally and bodily."* Every last instinct for self-preservation was gone. He stopped eating food, subsisting only on gin and opium and would stoop to any subterfuge to obtain them. The village children taunted him and tugged at his clothes which hung on his emaciated frame as he lurched across the cobblestones to and from the Black Bull Inn. When his old pub pal, Francis Grundy, visited him, he hardly recognized his old friend. He described Branwell as having…

> *"...a mass of red, unkempt, uncut hair, wildly floating round a great gaunt forehead; the cheeks yellow and hollow, the mouth fallen, the thin white lips not trembling but shaking, the sunken eyes, once small, now glaring."*

The townsfolk were used to seeing the parson's degenerate son teetering between the Parsonage and the Inn; so no one paid him much attention on Friday, September 22, 1847. But William Brown, the sexton's brother, noticed that Branwell was not only staggering but was gasping for breath. When he offered his help, Branwell was grateful for William's firm arm and together they slowly, carefully stumbled back to the Parsonage. Once home, Branwell went straight to bed, and a doctor was summoned. He had collapsed before, and there was no reason to expect that he would not again recover. However, the doctor's grave manner cast an air of finality into the room. There was nothing he could do. Branwell's years of self-abuse had taken too great a toll. Drink, drugs, and erratic eating had turned him into an old man even though he was only thirty-one years old.

Even more than the doctor's conclusion, it was Branwell's demeanor of surrender and defeat that forewarned what was to come. Rather than raving against his lost lover or the devil or *"the old man"* — his father — and threatening suicide, he was possessed with an eerie calm. His mind was clear and unclouded. He seemed returned to his *"natural affection[s]"* and spoke to his family with love and contrition. The following day, he asked for no drugs or alcohol and even managed to take in some food. His family may not have yet realized it, but Branwell sensed that his end was near. He seemed to have the courage to face his death with a calm clarity with which he was never able to face his life.

The next day, September 24, was a Sunday. While Emily, Charlotte, Anne and their father made their way through the graveyard to attend church, John Brown, the sexton, came to sit with Branwell in his sickbed. Suddenly, Branwell was seized with his old panic. He grasped John's hand and cried out, *"In all my past life I have done nothing either great or good. Oh John, I am dying!"* The sexton immediately called the family back. While his sisters looked on helplessly, Patrick held his only son in his arms and fervently prayed while Branwell uttered weak *"amens"* in concert with the old man's pleadings. When he felt Branwell's chest sink in as he exhaled his last breath, and fail to rise, Patrick *"cried out for the loss like David for that of Absalom – my son! My son – and refused at first to be comforted."* John Brown slipped silently out of the death room and climbed the church tower to toll the passing of Branwell Brontë.

Branwell had completed the painful round from prodigy to prodigal. Once the chief hope of his family, reduced to their chief disappointment and trial, he had finally returned to them with softness and remorse in his final hours. Yet failed potential and dissolution were the tragic legacy of his misspent life. Charlotte later reminisced,

> *"There is such a bitterness of pity for his life and death. Nothing remains of him but a memory of errors and sufferings. All his vices…are nothing now – we remember only his woes."*

Four black clad figures followed the plain wooden coffin in mournful procession to the church the following Thursday. They looked like ghostly silhouettes moving against a deep grey sky. A thin monotonous drizzle swamped the path. The muddy water soiled their clothes and soaked their shoes and feet. Emily shivered, her wet feet numbed on the cold stone floor throughout the service in the unheated church. When Branwell was laid to rest beneath the stones, next to his dead mother and two sisters, it was as if the heat had gone out of Emily, in both body and spirit. She never warmed again. In keeping with Haworth custom, a memorial service for Branwell was held on the first Sunday following his death. The date was October 1. It was the last day that Emily ever went out.

It was winter without and winter within for the last four members of the Brontë family. Grief sapped all creative impetus. No one had the heart to write. It was all they could do to just hold themselves and each other together. They all suffered physically as well as emotionally. Charlotte had headaches. Anne's asthma attacks became more frequent. Emily, historically the healthiest one in the family, was seized with a cold and cough that would not go away, and they all lost their appetites.

By the end of October, Charlotte sensed that something was gravely amiss with Emily. Something nameless and menacing had an iron grip on her. Deeply depressed, she had failed rapidly in the weeks following Branwell's death and was not rallying. She was not only refusing to eat, she was refusing to speak. Her cold persisted; yet, she refused to acknowledge that she was ailing. She refused to see a doctor and refused any remedy for relief. She insisted on performing all her household tasks and became irritated when anyone suggested that she rest or offered to help. The only chore she relinquished was walking her dogs. Perhaps this was most telling. Emily's love of the natural world was the overarching passion of her life. The earth was her primary muse and inspiration. Now, she even shut herself off from her beloved moors, where she had always found solace when human comfort failed her. No one and no thing could reach her or reason with her. She was beyond grief. She seemed to be in full retreat from life.

With every offer of help rebuffed, every expression of concern spurned, Charlotte was forced to stand by helplessly and watch her sister suffer in self-imposed silence and waste away. It was agonizing for her. She wrote to Ellen:

> *"Emily's cold and cough are very obstinate… She looks very, very thin and pale. Her reserved nature occasions me great uneasiness of mind. It is useless to question her; you get no answers. It is still more*

useless to recommend remedies; they are never adopted."

She echoed her frustration and concerns again in another letter to her editor, William Smith Williams:

"I would fain hope that Emily is a little better this evening, but it is difficult to ascertain this... she neither seeks nor will accept sympathy. To put any questions, to offer any aid, is to annoy...you must look on and see her do what she is unfit to do, and not dare to say a word."

In the passing weeks as Emily grew more frail and insubstantial, Charlotte grew more fearful and anxious. She did her best not to interfere. She knew her sister well:

"It is best usually to leave her to form her own judgment and especially not to advocate the side you wish her to favor; if you do, she is sure to lean in the opposite direction and ten to one will argue herself into non-compliance. Hitherto she has refused medicine, rejected medical advice; no reasoning, no entreaty, has availed to induce her to see a physician... I have again and again incurred her displeasure by urging the necessity of seeking advice, and I fear I must yet incur it again..."

Finally in desperation and in direct opposition to Emily's wishes, Charlotte called in a doctor. When Dr. Wheelhouse arrived at the parsonage, Emily refused to see him. Her two bewildered sisters apprehensively described, as best they could, Emily's symptoms. She was feverish and coughed incessantly, bringing up thick clumps of phlegm. She had pain in the chest and side and was gasping and panting at the slightest exertion. Dr. Wheelhouse left some medicine, but true to form, Emily refused to take anything from a *"poisoning doctor"* and insisted that *"Nature should be left to take her own course."*

Emily's body needed rest, warmth, food, medicine; yet, she denied it everything it needed to heal. It was as though she was enacting the death of Catherine Earnshaw, her title character in <u>Wuthering Heights</u>. She appeared to yearn for death, to be released from the *"shattered prison"* of her body, to be *"incomparably beyond and above"* her earthly existence. She was committing suicide by determined self-neglect and starvation.

Charlotte had to consider the unthinkable — that she would lose Emily. She wrote to Ellen:

> *"The tie of sister is near and dear indeed...her powerful and peculiar character only makes me cling to her more. Emily seems the nearest thing to my heart in this world."*

She kept Ellen updated on Emily's continual decline. She expressed the agony of her helplessness and the anguish of not knowing why Emily was rejecting her life:

> *"I believe if you were to see her, your impression would be that there is no hope. A more hollow, wasted, pallid aspect I have not beheld... The attack was, I believe in the first place, inflammation of the lungs; it ought to have been met promptly in time, but she would take no care, use no means. I do wish I knew her state of mind and feelings more clearly."*

As Emily descended further into starvation, she entered into a light-headed dreaminess that gave her a sensation of transcendence and ecstasy. This delusional mindset gave her a false sense of power and control. Strangely, as she became weakened in body, she became stronger in mind and more committed to her path. Emily's final symptom was the onset of diarrhea, which dehydrated her and caused *"continual thirst."* Undeterred, she even saw this as purifying.

On Monday, December 18, Emily went into the chilly hallway with an apronful of meat scraps and bread to feed the dogs. She stumbled weakly on the uneven flagstones. Charlotte and Anne were nearby and reached out to help her. Gasping for breath, she refused their outstretched arms and reached out *a "thin hand"* to steady herself against the wall and persisted in feeding the dogs herself.

Afterward, she tottered slowly back to the dining room where Charlotte and Anne were sitting near the fire with their needlework in a façade of normalcy. Emily sat down but was too weak to pick up her sewing. Charlotte put her project down and opened a volume of Emerson's Essays and read aloud until she found that Emily was not listening. She set the book aside, and they all went to bed early. As always, the stillness of the night was punctuated with Emily's coughing. Charlotte listened relentlessly and counted the hourly chimes on the clock waiting for morning to arrive.

Emily arose at her usual hour, seven a.m., her movements very slow and feeble now. Her sisters listened to her throat rattle with each breath as she slipped her dress onto her emaciated frame, not daring to offer to help her. Patrick, Charlotte and Anne looked at each other in silent despondence in the kitchen as they listened to her make her way down the stone staircase unaided. When she came in, their *"first glance at her face told [them] what would happen before night-fall."*

After sipping a bit of weak tea, she crossed the hallway into the parlor and went through the motions of picking up her sewing, but she dropped it back into her lap almost immediately out of sheer weakness. Charlotte did the only thing she could do. She sat at a desk across the room and poured out her anguish in a letter to Ellen:

> *"Dear Ellen – I should have written to you before, if I had had one word of hope to say; but I had not. She grows daily weaker. Moments as dark as these I have never known. I pray for God's support to us all... Yours faithfully-"*

She could not bear to stand by for one more hour listening to Emily's labored breathing and watching her vacant eyes while being forced by her sister's intractability to carry on a charade of normalcy. She was desperate to connect with her in some way, to offer a gift that would be accepted. Despairing, she paced the flagstone hall into the kitchen and stared out the back window at the wintry moors, the hoary frost of morning still clinging to the blades of frozen grass. Her earliest memories were with Emily on those gentle slopes. Then it came to her. Perhaps a sprig of heather would do. Surely Emily would not refuse that. She pulled a shawl over her shoulders and set out quickly to find a purple straggler, a leftover remnant of summer on the December hills. She scoured the moors for hours and finally found a small, withered spray that still retained a bit of color. With a sharp intake of breath, she snapped the branch and held it close to her chest and hurried back to the house on the hill, the *"sphere of her sorrows."*

By the time she reached home, Emily was delirious, muttering utterances that only she understood. Her eyes were *"dim and indifferent."* Like Catherine Earnshaw, she *"was all bewildered; she sighed, and moaned and knew nobody."* Charlotte knelt beside her, called her by name and laid the heather in her lap. But Emily was far away; she recognized neither the gift nor the giver. Charlotte motioned to Anne to help her move Emily to the couch. Emily was beyond resistance, and she moved lightly and easily between her sisters. As the three of them stepped to the sofa, the movement seemed to bring her back to them momentarily. As they eased her onto the sofa, her eyes met theirs in one last moment of recognition. Perhaps the stricken look of terror on her sisters' faces softened her at last, and she finally gave the permission she had withheld for so long:

"If you'll send for a doctor I'll see him now."

She laid back on the couch, closed her eyes, and she was gone. Keeper began to howl.

On the evening of Tuesday, December 19, the bell at St. Michael's church tolled the passing of the second Brontë, young and wasted, in less than three months. William Wood, the village carpenter, was called upon to make the coffin. When he took Emily's measurements, he said that he had never made so narrow a shell for an adult. It measured five feet seven inches in length and was a mere sixteen inches across.

On Friday, December 22, another solemn procession of four made their way between the Parsonage and the church behind a wooden coffin. This time, Keeper was at the head of the line. When they entered the church, Patrick Brontë gently directed Emily's dog into the family's box pew. There he stayed with them while Mr. Nicholls, Patrick's assistant curate, delivered the funeral service. He and the scattered villagers in the pews paid their respects to a woman they hardly knew. Perhaps the meager remnants of the Brontë family wondered if they knew her too, as they huddled together in their pew. They had lost the generous creative genius they knew on the day they had buried their brother. Who was the remote and skeletal creature that they had put into the narrow rectangle that would soon be lowered beneath the stones next to their mother, brother, and two sisters?

It seemed that the world had literally lost its color without Emily in it. The earth was a silent, deathly white outside the walls of the Parsonage. The inhabitants inside wore the silent, deathly black of grief. Keeper sat outside Emily's door and howled for weeks. Charlotte obsessively recalled the details of Emily's death, trying to understand why she had *"made haste to leave us?"* The answer was simple for the loyal servants of the Brontë family, Martha Brown and her sisters. Emily had died of grief for her brother. *"They were all well when Mr. Branwell was buried,"* Martha told Mrs. Gaskell, the first Brontë biographer. *"But Miss Emily broke down the next week."* She was dead within three months.

On Christmas Eve, Charlotte sat alone near the slow embers of a late night fire and lamplight and tried to articulate her sorrow.   Her poem of lamentation and hope speaks directly to Emily:

> *My darling thou wilt never know*
> *The grinding agony of woe*
> *That we have borne for thee...*
>
> *The nightly anguish thou art spared*
> *When all the crushing truth is bared...*
> *When the galled heart is pierced with grief,*
> *Till wildly it implores relief...*
>
> *Weary, weary, dark and drear,*
> *How shall I the journey bear,*
> *The burden and the distress*
> *[Of] life's lone wilderness.*
>
> *Then since thou art spared such pain*
> *We will not wish thee here again;*
> *He that lives must mourn.*
> *God help us through our misery*
> *And give us rest and joy with thee...*

Anne also sought relief in her grief with these simple lines:

> *Oh thou has taken my delight*
> *And hope of life away*
> *And bid me watch the painful night*
> *And wait the weary day.*

It was difficult for Emily's family to understand and impossible to accept that she would will herself out of this world—away from the natural world that she felt kin to on an organic level—away from the family that she loved. Yet, she was a spiritual and sensitive person who had always lived with one foot in the next world.

Emily's solitary and visionary nature allowed her to simultaneously live in both worlds — seen and unseen. Both were equally valid for her. She often expressed in her poetry a preference for the unseen world where she experienced ecstasy rather than the uncertainty caused by the fickle frailty of humanity. She used fasting to enhance her access to the unseen world and to induce visions. Perhaps she was attempting to assuage her emotional destitution after the loss of Branwell by using the tools of isolation and fasting that had served her before. This may have been the reason why she refused to acknowledge any illness and to reject all efforts to reach her. She was using physical deprivation to propel her into a vision quest where she hoped to find relief.

Her practiced isolation and preference for the immaterial world created a self-sufficiency that made it perhaps not so difficult for her to leave her material home and loved ones. She had been contemplating death for years in her poems and prose. Death was the ultimate resolution to the conflict of Catherine and Heathcliff in *Wuthering Heights*. Now it seemed it was the ultimate resolution for her life. She believed death to be the great equalizer, joining material and immaterial, good and evil, love and hate, lowly and lofty, all into one great universal soul. She did not fear it. She even yearned for it. Now she was one with it...

> *O for the time when I shall sleep*
> *Without identity,*
> *And never care how rain may steep*
> *Or snow may cover me! . . .*
> *O let me die, that power and will*
> *Their cruel strife may close,*
> *And vanquished Good, victorious Ill*
> *Be lost in one repose.*

After Emily

Two tragic deaths, premature and senseless, in the space of three months took a sharp toll on Charlotte and Anne. Anne caught influenza over Christmas and could not seem to shake it. In early January, her father called in a physician from Leeds who diagnosed her with consumption, a death sentence for a Brontë. Yet, Anne took the news with her characteristic equanimity and grace. Unlike her sister, she took all of the doctor's recommendations and did everything possible to regain her health. Even so, she felt *"a dreadful darkness closing in… death standing at the gate."* Charlotte was so consumed by her *"blank… and bitter"* grief over the loss of Emily that she was nearly numb to Anne's sinking health. Anne dealt with the reality of her terminal illness very much alone and in stoic silence.

In May, Anne was so weak that she was in a wheelchair. Charlotte and Ellen decided to take her to the coast with the hope that the fresh sea air would ease her symptoms and give her a chance to live. They bade goodbye to Papa on May 24, 1849, and made their way to Scarborough by way of York. At Anne's request, Charlotte and Ellen wheeled her through the magnificent York Minster before they moved on to Scarborough.

The three arrived at Scarborough on Saturday, May 26. Anne was dead by Monday afternoon, May 28. Her last whispered words were to her sister, *"Take courage, Charlotte."* She was twenty-nine years old.

Charlotte chose to *"lay the flower where it had fallen"* and buried Anne in Scarborough rather than take her back to

Haworth for her final sleep with the rest of her family under the stones at St. Michael's. There were three mourners at Anne's funeral, Charlotte, Ellen and Anne's former schoolmistress, Miss Wooler from Roe Head, who happened to be in Scarborough.

Charlotte had lost three siblings in eight months time. She was the only one left. When she returned to the Parsonage, Papa implored her, *"You must bear me up. I shall sink if you fail me."* They were both stunned by the enormity of their tragedy and desolation. They comforted each other as best they could, but locked in a father/daughter dynamic of authority and obedience, and a family pattern of profound reserve, they suffered silently and separately. Papa closeted himself in his study, as he always had. Charlotte stayed in the dining room across the hall:

> *"The great trial is in the evenings. We used to assemble in the dining room. We used to talk. Now I sit by myself – remembering their suffering – what they said and did – how they looked in mortal affliction….A dreary calm reigns in the midst of which we seek resignation."*

Finding herself profoundly alone, she penned the pathos of her grief in letters to her confidants. To William Smith Williams she wrote:

> *"…a year ago – had a prophet warned me how I should stand in June 1849 – how stripped and bereaved – had he foretold the autumn, the winter, the spring of sickness and suffering to be gone through – I should have thought – this can never be endured. It is over. Branwell – Emily – Anne are gone like dreams – gone as Maria and Elizabeth went twenty years ago. One*

> by one, I have watched them fall asleep on my arm – and closed their glazed eyes – I have seen them buried one by one."

Emily's death weighed heaviest on her. Of it, she added an extra lament:

> "Anne's quiet, Christian death did not rend my heart as Emily's stern, simple, undemonstrative end did. I let Anne go to God and felt he had a right to her... I could hardly let Emily go. I wanted to hold her back then, and I want her back now."

Part of her grieving process was to rework the novel she had started the year before, *Shirley*. She employed her old Angrian tactic of *"making all alive again."* Using Emily as her inspiration, she told Mrs. Gaskell that Shirley was *"what Emily Brontë would have been had she been placed in health and prosperity."* Shirley, like Emily, was authoritative and self-assured. She whistled like a man, knew how to shoot, loved her dogs, cauterized her own wounds, wrote essays in French and experienced revelatory trances on the moors. Creating this literary tribute to her dead sister *"took me out of a dark and desolate reality into an unreal but happier region."*

Patrick Brontë assuaged his grief by taking action. In the year following Anne's death, he gathered two hundred twenty-two signatures and petitioned the General Board of Health to look into the deplorable unsanitary conditions of Haworth which caused such a high mortality rate. This led to the Babbage Report, a very detailed account of conditions at Haworth that recommended a clean water supply for the town. Patrick pestered the General Board of Health for six years before the needed changes were made.

Without her sisters' companionship at home, Charlotte broke the lonely tedium by traveling to London from time to time and hobnobbing with other artists and authors of the day. But the journeys always caused her headaches and nervous exhaustion. When she returned home to recuperate, she would be overcome by extreme loneliness in the empty house. There was little relief from pain, physically or emotionally. She tried to warm up the parsonage, which had only ever had white walls and curtainless windows, by putting up drapes and wallpaper. She paid for the improvements with her own money from earnings from her books. Finally, she went back to writing to fill the gaping void and wrote her fourth and final book, <u>Villette</u>.

Not long after she finished the book, she heard a reluctant rap on the dining room door on a December evening. She opened it to find her father's assistant curate, Arthur Bell Nicholls, standing in the hallway in an obvious state of agitation. His face was drained of color, and he was visibly shaking. In a faltering voice, he declared his love for her and asked her to marry him. He had fully expected to be rejected by her, and he was surprised when she said that she would speak to her father.

At thirty-eight years old, Charlotte approached her father timidly about Arthur's proposal. Patrick was enraged and offended that an assistant curate would have the audacity to even dream of marrying his daughter. He was vehemently against the union. In deference to her father's wishes, Charlotte turned down what would surely have been her last chance for love and companionship. Arthur promptly left the Parsonage in dejected disgrace for another parish. Within months of his departure, he and Charlotte were corresponding. Charlotte was genuinely affected by the depth and urgency of Arthur's love in his letters. As Patrick watched his daughter warm with each heartfelt missive, he finally begrudgingly gave his permission for the two to become engaged in April.

The couple planned their wedding for June 29 at eight o'clock in the morning. But Charlotte's joy was dampened the night before when her father announced that he would not attend the ceremony. Hence, Miss Wooler once again filled the family vacancy and stood up to give the bride away. Ellen Nussey sat alone in the family pew.

The couple went on a honeymoon to Ireland for six weeks and by the time they returned to live in the Parsonage, Charlotte had discovered that she loved being Arthur's wife. After enduring five long years of loneliness, she treasured *"the affectionate devotion of a truthful, honourable man."* She cherished the meals they shared, their long walks on the moors and talks by the evening fire. But her newfound contentment was to be short-lived. By late December, she was pregnant. She would not live to know the joys of motherhood as well.

Charlotte's pregnancy brought on severe nausea and recurring faintness. Unable to keep any food or liquid down, she weakened and wasted daily, becoming dehydrated and feverish. Arthur tended to her devotedly. She wrote:

> *"I find in my husband the tenderest nurse, the kindest support, the best earthly comfort that ever woman had. His patience never fails, and it is tried by sad days and broken nights."*

Having watched her brother and four sisters waste away and perish, she feared the worst, but clung to the hope of life for love of her husband and unborn child. By March, she was floating between sleep and delirium. One afternoon, she awakened to see her husband kneeling by her bed, holding her hands in his own, and heard his urgent prayer to God pleading for her life. *"Oh!"* she murmured, *"I am not going to die, am I? He will not separate us, we have been so happy."*

Married for just nine months and expecting her first child, Charlotte Brontë died on March 31, 1855, in the same bed in which she had been born. It had also been her wedding bed, her parents' wedding bed, and the bed where her mother, her two young sisters and her Aunt had died years before. Charlotte was thirty-nine years old when she and her unborn child joined the rest of her family beneath the stones of St. Michael's.

Patrick Brontë had now outlived his entire family. He survived for six more years at the Parsonage with his assistant curate and son-in-law, Arthur. They lived as the inhabitants of the Parsonage always had, *"ever near but ever separate."* In August 1860, Patrick preached his last sermon at St. Michael's, then took to his bed in the room overlooking the graveyard. The white haired old man remained there, *"his mental faculties unimpaired,"* well cared for by his old servants and Arthur, throughout the fall, winter and spring. When he died on June 7, 1861, it was not a peaceful passing. The Haworth doctor entered the cause of death on the death certificate as *"chronic bronchitis; dyspepsia, convulsions, duration nine hours."* Patrick Brontë was eighty-four years old.

When he joined the rest of his family in the silent vault beneath the stones of St. Michael's, the arduous journey Patrick that had begun as an obscure fiery haired and hot-headed Irish peasant with an audacious dream of a life beyond his inheritance of poverty and illiteracy came to an end. He had dared to leave his home and family to pursue his own Pilgrim's Progress for a glorious reward. He had changed his name to better suit his ambitions to write something brilliant, to inspire a flock of *"sick and sinning parishioners,"* to marry above his station and have sons who would change the world with their golden gifts. Despite his grand ambitions of fame and gentility, his dreams dissolved piece by piece in an obscure outback parish. His verses forgotten, his wife dead, his only son miserably failed, two daughters dead in childhood and his three remaining daughters dying childless, all ensured he would not only be the first Brontë but he would also be the last.

His family had flashed into the world *"comet-like in its course"* with lives *"so stormy and so brief."* Though they weathered a *"Wild morn...and doubtful noon/But yet it was a glorious sun,"* Emily wrote. Yet, not even in the boundless imagination of their writing could they have foreseen the scope of Brontë immortality.

Years before, heaven had presaged not one, but three glorious suns. While Emily, Charlotte and Anne were still writing their first novels, they went walking on the moors one day with their friend, Ellen, when *"a sudden change and light came into the sky."*

"Look!" exclaimed Charlotte, pointing to three suns shining clearly overhead. The four women stood a little while, gazing skyward, silently marveling at a beautiful parhelion, a rare solar phenomenon which occurs when

"mock suns" are reflected through the prism of the sun's halo. When Ellen turned back to her three friends, their faces incandescent in the rainbow hued light, she was suddenly struck with a premonition. She knew in that moment that the Brontë sisters would live forever…

"That is you!" she burst out. *"You are the three suns!"*

When Patrick began his journey, he could never have envisioned that the bleak house of his lost dreams and tragic end would one day shine with the eternal brightness of three suns. For centuries to come, his Parsonage would be a hallowed shrine where millions of pilgrims would come from all over the world to pay homage to the lives and legacies of his three plain, shy daughters—the brilliant Brontë sisters.

Emily as a Poet

Though she is most well known for her final literary work, the novel Wuthering Heights, Emily is considered one of the greatest poets who ever lived. Wuthering Heights has been described as *"the masterpiece of a poet rather than the hybrid creation of the novelist."* In her timeless tale, she succeeds in translating her poetic gift of finding the divine mysteries of life in the ordinary... snow, hearth fire, gate, wind, stable, heath, blossom... to her prose. Emily entwined the human drama with the atmosphere of the seasons — particularly storms and darkness as she deals with the principles of life, death, love and immortality. The result is nothing less than poetry in prose.

From the time she was very small, Emily perceived a spirit world just beyond sight. When she was just six years old, she went out *"to take an airing on the moors"* on a fine early September day with Branwell, Anne and two family servants. While they were out, a sudden storm came up. It was so violent that Patrick compared it to an earthquake afterwards. Anxiously watching from his back windows in hopes of seeing his children hurrying home, Patrick saw huge, dark storm clouds blot out the sun as they marched over the horizon as if they had been called to attack. He literally saw the windowpanes and the floorboards of the Parsonage heave as the storm broke. It was a terrifying ordeal as the earth literally trembled under lashing rain and pummeling thunder. Unbeknownst to Patrick, the children and servants had found shelter at a nearby farm. When they returned home, everyone was shaken by the suddenness and violence of the storm except for little Emily, who appeared to be delighted with the entire experience. Forever after she was addicted to storms. She found in nature's untamed elements the presence of spirits calling to her own. She felt kindred to the raw and rugged nature they found on the thorny, heathered hills. Nature was the muse of her imagination, her inspiration, her guide and her spiritual resource.

Loud without the wind was roaring
Through th'autumnal sky;
Drenching wet, the cold rain pouring,
Spoke of winter nigh.

All too like that dreary eve,
Did my exiled spirit grieve.
Grieved at first, but grieved not long,
Sweet--how softly sweet!--it came;
Wild words of an ancient song,
Undefined, without a name.

God's Singers

"It was spring, and the skylark was singing:"
Those words they awakened a spell;
They unlocked a deep fountain, whose springing,
Nor absence, nor distance can quell.

In the gloom of a cloudy November
They uttered the music of May;
They kindled the perishing ember
Into fervour that could not decay.

Awaken, o'er all my dear moorland,
West-wind, in thy glory and pride!
Oh! call me from valley and lowland,
To walk by the hill-torrent's side!

It is swelled with the first snowy weather;
The rocks they are icy and hoar,
And sullenly waves the long heather,
And the fern leaves are sunny no more.

But lovelier than corn-fields all waving
In emerald, and vermeil, and gold,
Are the heights where the north-wind is raving,
And the crags where I wandered of old.

For the moors! For the moors, where the short grass
Like velvet beneath us should lie!
For the moors! For the moors, where each high pass
Rose sunny against the clear sky!

For the moors, where the linnet was trilling
Its song on the old granite stone;
Where the lark, the wild sky-lark, was filling
Every breast with delight like its own!

Emily Brontë

What language can utter the feeling
Which rose, when in exile afar,
On the brow of a lonely hill kneeling,
I saw the brown heath growing there?

The spirit which bent 'neath its power,
How it longed--how it burned to be free!
If I could have wept in that hour,
Those tears had been heaven to me.

Well--well; the sad minutes are moving,
Though loaded with trouble and pain;
And some time the loved and the loving
Shall meet on the mountains again!

One of her first poems, from when she was about age eighteen, documents an ecstatic experience on the moors at night:

...A little child
Strayed from its father's cottage door,
And in the hour of moonlight wild
Laid lonely on the desert moor.

I heard it then, you heard it too,
And seraph sweet it sang to you;
But like the shriek of misery
That wild, wild music wailed to me.

Her spiritual nature and sensitivity allowed her to perceive the animation of the natural world in a supernatural way. She wrote as she lived, on two parallel planes –the material and the spiritual. She found access to the spiritual most easily at night.

God's Singers

Released from the demands of day, she could lie on her cot in the quiet privacy of darkness and follow the tracks of planets, stars, moon and meteors through her curtainless window. In the immensity of space, she was freed from the bright bars of day and evolved into a poet of the night:

Stars

All through the night, your glorious eyes
Were gazing down in mine,
And with a full heart's thankful sighs
I blessed that watch divine!

I was at peace, and drank your beams
As they were life to me
And revelled in my changeful dreams
Like petrel on the sea.

Thought followed thought, star followed star
Through boundless regions on,
While one sweet influence, near and far,
Thrilled through and proved us one.

Why did the morning dawn to break
So great, so pure a spell,
And scorch with fire the tranquil cheek
Where your cool radiance fell?

Blood-red the rose, and arrow-straight
His fierce beams struck my brow:
The soul of Nature sprang elate,
But mine sank sad and low!

Emily Brontë

My lids closed down, yet through their veil
I saw him blazing still;
And steep in gold the misty dale
And flash upon the hill.

I turned me to the pillow then
To call back Night, and see
Your worlds of solemn light, again
Throb with my heart and me!

It would not do the pillow glowed
And glowed both roof and floor,
And birds sang loudly in the wood,
And fresh winds shook the door.

The curtains waved, the wakened flies
Were murmuring round my room,
Imprisoned there, till I should rise
And give them leave to roam.

O Stars and Dreams and Gentle Night;
O Night and Stars return!
And hide me from the hostile light
That does not warm, but burn

That drains the blood of suffering men;
Drinks tears, instead of dew;
Let me sleep through his blinding reign,
And only wake with you!

All Day I've Toiled

All day I've toiled but not with pain
In learning's golden mine
And now at eventide again
The moonbeams softly shine

There is no snow upon the ground
No frost on wind or wave
The south wind blew with gentlest sound
And broke their icy grave

'Tis sweet to wander here at night
To watch the winter die
With heart as summer sunshine light
And warm as summer's sky

O may I never lose the peace
That lulls me gently now
Though time should change my youthful face
And years should shade my brow

True to myself and true to all
May I be healthful still
And turn away from passion's call
And curb my own wild will

Given to solitude and darkness, and pathologically shy to the point of being a mystery at times even to her own family, Emily Brontë has been called The Sphinx of Literature. However, her aversion to society did not spring from misanthropy; rather, from an intense inner life that must be guarded at all costs lest the charm be broken, her thread of narrative lost. Truth was her oxygen. She had no patience for social niceties. She went straight to the heart of every matter, both living and writing, in an uncomplicated, laconic style, as in this excerpt from "The Philosopher:"

> *So said I, and still say the same;*
> *--Still to my Death will say —*
> *Three gods, within this little frame,*
> *Are warring night and day.*
> *Heaven could not hold them all, and yet*
> *They all are held in me;*
> *And must be mine till I forget*
> *My present entity!*
> *Oh! For the time, when in my breast*
> *Their struggles will be o'er!*
> *Oh, for the day, when I shall rest,*
> *And never suffer more!*

In the final analysis, Emily and her sisters did more than pen a few poems-- their writing redeemed their lives of tragedy with purpose. They became the salvation of their father and their publishers as well as breaking ground for women writers for all time. Most of all, they left timeless works that continue to touch and inspire endless generations of readers.

The Novels of the Brontës

Charlotte	**Emily**	**Anne**
Currer Bell	*Ellis Bell*	*Acton Bell*
<u>The Professor</u>	<u>Wuthering Heights</u>	<u>Agnes Grey</u>
<u>Jane Eyre</u>	Finest woman poet	<u>The Tenant of</u>
<u>Shirley</u>	in English	<u>Wildfell Hall</u>
<u>Villette</u>	literature	

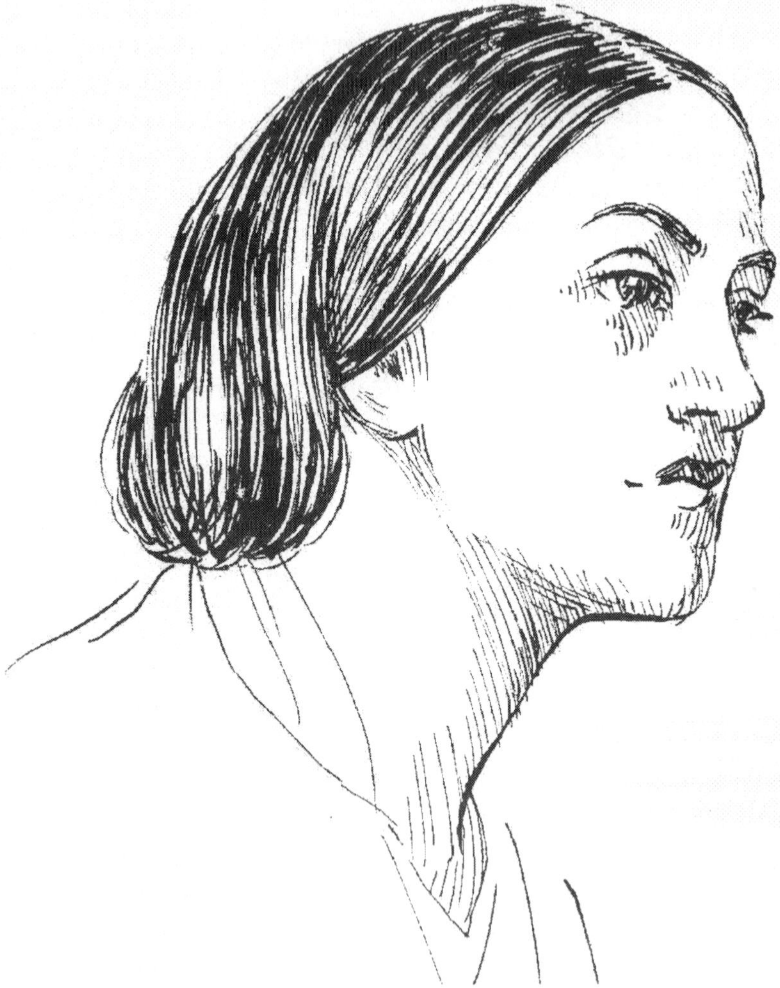

Christina Georgiana Rossetti
1830 – 1894

The bleak midwinter day was more grey than white...

Snow had fallen, snow on snow, snow upon snow...

A small, dark figure sat writing at a narrow desk, pallid against the wintry sky. The scratch of her pen, starting and stopping, splintered the deathly stillness of the room...

Earth stood hard as iron, Water like a stone...

She had known too many Decembers in her life — years of Decembers...

What can I give him? Poor as I am...

How deep her heart burned with love for her Lord! But He was a harsh God. He hated everything she loved. She yearned to break the yoke of human passion — to burn with the pure white heat of a saint. Instead, her heart merely glowed with the fire of a poet.

Christina Rossetti was born on a cold December day into a world of stark polarities — a divided soul into a divided world. England's once unscathed green hills were pocked with *"dark satanic mills"* that oozed unchecked filth. The gap between humanity and machinery, city and country, rich and poor, science and religion was straining the English reserve.

Amidst this English moil was a thriving community of Italian expatriates. Among them was Christina's father, a poet and Dante scholar named Gabriele Rossetti, who had fled political oppression in his native country. In England, he became a professor of Italian at King's College. He lived for a time with the family of a colleague and fellow political refugee, Gaetano Polidori—a lovable, erudite eccentric with a rich store of knowledge and experience. He was present at the fall of The Bastille and was disgusted with the entire affair. During the melee, a sword was thrust into his hands to dispose of any nearby aristocrats. Instead, he gave it away on the next street corner to the first unarmed Frenchman he came upon.

Gaetano was married to an English governess named Anna. They were the parents of four sons and four daughters, the most notable of whom was their son John, author of *The Vampyre*, (the first vampire story written in English), and personal friend and physician to Lord Byron. Their daughter, Frances, was twenty-three years old when she caught the eye of their middle aged houseguest, Gabriele, age forty-three. Frances Polidori was a sturdy woman with a quick wit, who, having been born and bred in England, was more English than Italian in her character. Her strongest characteristic was that she had a decidedly evangelical Anglican bent. In spite of their twenty year age difference and Gabriele's religion, Frances returned his affections. They were married on a fresh spring day in April, 1826. To appease both of their religious preferences, they held two ceremonies, two days apart, one Catholic and one Anglican.

Gabriele and Frances were devoted to each other. Gabriele never naturalized himself as an Englishman or converted to Anglicanism, but he frequently publicized his opposition to pretentious papistry. Having an independent minded father and a devout mother would have a profound effect on all the Rossetti children who were born in quick succession — four children in four years. The youngest was our poet, Christina.

- February, 1827 - Maria Francesca
- May, 1828 - Gabriel Charles Dante
- September, 1829 - William Michael
- December, 1830 - Christina Georgiana

The children, being close in age, were each other's playmates and allies. Their mother mused, *"All the children are the same size so it's as easy to bring up four as one."* This is a pattern common to the families of all our poets — several children being born very close together, creating unusually strong sibling bonds in families with distinctly unique identities.

Wrapped in Italian culture and speaking both Italian and English, the Rossetti household was a vibrant place that was full of academics, arts and politics. There were endless comings and goings of Italian exiles of all sorts — from patriots, politicians, aristocrats, literary men, and musicians to gardeners and organ grinders. In the evenings, they crowded together in the sitting room to lament the state of their country, discuss art, literature and subtle interpretations of Dante — hands, voices and emotions rising and falling with Italian passion. It was like a fiery little Italian isle in a sea of British society. The Rossetti children were never shushed out of the room or shielded from the adult drama. They played on the hearth rug by firelight in the center of the discussion, soaking up the spirited atmosphere of intellect, language, art and ideas.

Their holidays were spent at their Polidori grandparents' country estate, Holmer Green, in Buckinghamshire. The six hour journey, made by stagecoach, was always a big event. There, they enjoyed the love and adoration of their grandparents and maiden aunts, Charlotte and Eliza. The city-dwelling Rossetti's spent many happy hours there. They had full access to their grandfather's library where they read Milton, in both English and Italian, Shakespeare, Shelley, Byron, Keats, and the Italian poetry of Petrarch and Dante. The children explored the wilderness and nurtured their love of nature. Christina later remembered the penetrating effect that these countryside rambles had on her:

> *"If any one thing schooled me in the direction of poetry, it was perhaps the delightful idle liberty to prowl all alone about my grandfather's cottage grounds."*

She later memorialized the experience poetically:

> *Before green apples blush,*
> *Before green nuts embrown,*
> *Why, one day in the country*
> *Is worth a month in town.*

They all began authorship while they were still children. Though their childhood literary adventures did not rival the Brontë children's Angria and Gondal sagas, they produced an illustrated family magazine called "Hodge Podge." Many of their ideas for stories and poems were taken from books of verse read to them by their mother and by their intellectually charged environment. They challenged each other to create sonnets using given rhymes, developing their technical skills for verse early on. Christina had a natural propensity for words and a knack for putting them together in a melodic and metered way. She was creating poetry before she could even write. When she was just four years old, she dictated her first two line poem to her mother. It is not a rhyme but it is perfectly metered:

> *"Cecilia never went to school*
> *Without her gladiator."*

When her precocious children were grown and well known, Frances quipped, *"Yes, my children all have talent, great talent; I only wish they had a little common sense."* Maria, the oldest, was sober and devout. From the time she was thirteen years old, she wanted to be a nun.

The oldest son, Gabriel, who later chose to call himself Dante Gabriel, had an impulsive, artistic personality. His first sketches showed such talent that by the time he was five years old the family decided he should be trained as an artist. He has been compared to Branwell Brontë because he lived a very egocentric life and died early of dissipation. He far exceeded Branwell's accomplishments, however, and created a beautiful body of work. He had a dramatic effect on the art world before he died.

The next son, William, was the most gentle of all the children. He was staid and dependable, perhaps in compensation for the irresponsibility of his older brother. Even though all the Rossetti children were close, William seemed to be able to see right into the soul of Christina. From the time she sought refuge with him as a child to escape Dante Gabriel's teasing, he was her champion. Eventually, he would become Christina's first biographer.

Christina was even more fractious in temperament than Dante Gabriel. Their mother, Frances, called them her *"two storms,"* and Maria and William her *"two calms."* Christina was highly sensitive, emotional, creative, and had a volatile temper. As she grew older, she would dangerously turn this temper inward on herself.

When Christina entered adolescence, she began to adopt her mother's piety and evangelism — in the extreme. She was educated entirely at home by her mother, her devout sister and her two pious maiden aunts. Her only outside influence was the Reverend Mr. Dodsworth of Christ Church. The core of their education for Christina was a morality based on self-denial, humility and the suppression of vanity. She took their teachings to heart and underwent a dramatic metamorphosis in which she began to repress her spontaneity, vivacity and passion. She began by changing her actions in the hope of changing her nature which she believed was deeply flawed. She affected extreme politeness. In fact, William told her that *"she would soon become so polite it would be impossible to live with her."*

Elizabeth Barrett Browning, who fled England for Italy, described the effect of an English education on the Italian temperament as being *"pricked to a pattern with a pin."* In later life, Christina reminisced on the nature of her English education in comparison with an Italian friend:

> *We Englishwomen, trim, correct,*
> *All minted in the selfsame mould,*
> *Warm-hearted but of semblance cold,*
> *All-courteous out of self-respect.*

Christina Rossetti

> *She, woman in her natural grace,*
> *Less trammeled she by lore of school,*
> *Courteous by nature not by rule,*
> *Warm-hearted and of cordial face.*

Christina stopped wearing her hair down in long dark ringlets and began pulling it back into a severe buns twisted and pinned in headphone fashion on the sides of her head. She adopted the sober style of her mother and dressed plainly in dark colors. She denied herself little enjoyments such as playing chess, a game she loved. Losing made her furious and the pleasure of winning made her prideful, so she gave it up. She refused to go to the theater because she did not want to endorse the lax morals of the actors.

The self-imposed process of obedience was painful. She began a lifelong struggle of feeling pulled between two discordant sides of herself—her passion and her piety. Not being able to eradicate her human passions that she deemed hateful and sinful, she poured them into her piety. However, often being overwrought by the tension of her inner polarities, she was frequently unwell in body as well as in spirit. It is not surprising that this is when her health problems began. Her two main physical complaints were sensations of choking or suffocating and sharp pains in her chest and arms. The doctor who attended her when she was fifteen diagnosed her with *"religious mania."* William wrote that by the time Christina was sixteen, she had become a *"sadly smitten invalid."* He described the change in her personality in a particularly descriptive way:

> *"Her temperament and character, naturally warm and free, became a fountain sealed."*

A dim light was beginning to dawn in the medical field about the connection between social repression and nervous illness in women. Charles Mercier stated that *"few women passed through adolescence without some form of hysteria caused by lack of an outlet for...emotional and sexual [development]."* Freud theorized that *"repetitious domestic routines could be the cause of hysteria in very intelligent women."* The frequency of psychosomatic illness among nineteenth century women is staggering.

Christina's poetry began to take on themes of being caged and stifled. In her poem "A Royal Princess," the following lines are found:

> *Two and two my guards behind, two and two before*
> *Two and two on either hand, they guard me evermore,*
> *Me, poor dove that must not coo —*
> *Eagle that must not soar.*

Kathleen Jones, a Rossetti biographer, surmises that *"only the soul of [a] poet could escape the cage"* of Victorian womanhood. Christina could not escape her cage because it was self-imposed. She continued to sing from behind the bars, but the songs were sad. Even though she was pressed to restrain her natural passions, her family continued to encourage her writing, which was not a widely accepted female activity. Her grandfather helped her to launch her literary career when he self-published a book of her poems when she was in her early teens. This parallels Elizabeth Barrett Browning's first book of poetry which was published in her early teens by her father.

This entire family of creative spirits keenly felt this earthly/heavenly divide. It is interesting to note how they each responded to it. True to their passionate, artistic natures, they all went to extremes. While Christina practiced a life of asceticism, Maria eventually became an Anglican nun. William and Dante Gabriel, however, took the opposite path and rejected organized religion all together. Dante Gabriel's path was the most flamboyant.

The family resources were being dedicated to sending him to the Royal Academy for artistic training. Young artists were taught by copying old masters. New methods and innovations were looked upon with suspicion. Dante Gabriel and his friends, Holman Hunt and John Millais, found this atmosphere to be stuffy and tiresome. They believed they had to go back to art before Raphael, who they felt had set a precedence for *"pompous posturing,"* to rediscover truth in artistic expression. They took their youthful energy and idealism and left the Royal Academy.

They embraced early Italian painting because they admired the subjects' *"naïve traits of frank expression and unaffected grace."* They reached back to the purity and simplicity of art in the Middle Ages, a time before society was corrupted by industrialization and materialism. They became enamored with the high romantic ideals of the Arthurian legends. Dante Gabriel particularly liked to paint chivalric *"knights rescuing ladies, lovers in medieval dress"* and scenes from the romantic poets. Their subjects, though projecting an ideal, would be painted with absolute attention to realistic detail. This brought their style to a unique hybrid of realism and idealism that was a new style of art.

They hotly debated the name they would give to their movement. They settled on a name which would be known only to them—the Pre-Raphaelite Brotherhood. They agreed to affix the initials P.R.B. to their names on their canvases. But its meaning was to be kept secret. Their little group was taking on the character of a secret society. They decided to limit the membership of their Brotherhood to the mystical number seven. Thomas Woolner, a sculptor, Frederick Stephens and James Collinson, painters, joined the P.R. B., and William Rossetti was admitted as the group's historian. Collinson and Woolner were the oldest at twenty-three; Millais and William the youngest at nineteen.

They painted together at each other's houses and started a reading circle. They read the Brontë sisters' novels and discussed their merits along with the rest of London. *Jane Eyre* found greater favor because it held to high ideals. Dante Gabriel was disturbed by *Wuthering Heights*. He said it was *"a fiend of book. The action is laid in hell."* They embraced the words of John Ruskin who espoused that truth was to be found in nature. They discovered the poetry of Keats, who was not well known at the time. They read Shelley and Tennyson and painted scenes from their poems. They sometimes included the verses of the poem into the scene or on the frame, blending art and poetry in a way that has rarely been equaled.

The P.R.B. also produced a journal titled, "The Germ, Thoughts towards Nature In Poetry, Literature, and Art." It was a collection of poetry and prose, critique and artistic etchings. It was printed by Aylott & Jones, the same printers that produced the Brontë sisters' first collection of poems. Christina published seven poems in it under the pseudonym, Ellen Alleyne, a pen-name chosen for her by Dante Gabriel. She was also the group's first regular model, making her an unofficial member of the P.R.B.

She was the type of beauty that appealed to the Pre-Raphaelite painters. She had delicately chiseled features, an abundance of hair, wide lustrous eyes, a willowy neck and natural purity and simplicity. As befitted her religiosity, she was the model for several of Dante Gabriel's paintings of the Madonna. She was well suited to the subject—modest yet attractive. But it was Christina's personal piety that Dante Gabriel captured in his powerful depictions of the Virgin Mother. To look at portraits of Christina is to feel that she was born a mystic—her deep, dark eyes seem to be filled with inward vision.

The P.R.B. provided Christina with a social and artistic outlet, but the most profound effect it had on her was that it introduced her to her first love, the painter James Collinson, when she was seventeen years old. James was also a person of deep devotion who painted mostly religious themes. Undoubtedly, this spirit of similar devotion drew James and Christina together. James had been reared in the Church of England, but he had converted to Catholicism before meeting Christina. This created an insurmountable problem when he proposed to her following their two year romance. Though she had been reared in a home with parents of differing faiths, she recognized that James was a much more devout Catholic than her father had ever been. This caused her concern for their future children growing up in a home with parents of conflicting religious convictions. After much agonized soul searching, she decided that she could not marry someone who was not of her faith, no matter how much she loved him.

When she tearfully told him of her resolve, James was thrown into a search of his own soul. He reconsidered his earlier conversion and decided that his Catholic convictions were not incompatible with Anglicanism. He reverted to the faith of his childhood and proposed to Christina again—this time as an Anglican. Being very much in love with him, she was overjoyed and immediately accepted. From then on, her brother William remembered, she *"freely and warmly bestowed her affections on him."*

Filled with the ardor of first love, Christina penned one of her loveliest, most joyful poems:

A Birthday

My heart is like a singing bird
　Whose nest is in a water'd shoot;
My heart is like an apple-tree
　Whose boughs are bent with thick-set fruit;
My heart is like a rainbow shell
　That paddles in a halcyon sea;
My heart is gladder than all these,
　Because my love is come to me.

Raise me a daïs of silk and down;
　Hang it with vair and purple dyes;
Carve it in doves and pomegranates,
　And peacocks with a hundred eyes;
Work it in gold and silver grapes,
　In leaves and silver fleurs-de-lys;
Because the birthday of my life
　Is come, my love is come to me.

James had a weak and indecisive character. William described him as a *"man of timorous conscience."* After months of religious doubt, he felt compelled to revert to Catholicism once again. He broke off his engagement to Christina and left the P.R.B. He sold his paints and entered a Jesuit college to train for the priesthood. However, he left the Jesuits when he was consigned to scrubbing the shoes of the other contemplatives *"as an apprenticeship in humility."* He later married Eliza Herbert, sister-in-law of another Pre-Raphaelite brother.

William recalled that this was *"a staggering blow at Christina Rossetti's peace of mind on the very threshold of womanly life, and a blow from which she did not fully recover for years."* She had yielded her heart to romantic love for the first time, completely and with commitment, as was her nature. Steadfast in self-restraint, we will never know the tears she shed over her heartbreak with James. She was extremely secretive about her true feelings and affections. William wrote that *"it would have been both indelicate and futile to press her with inquiries."* In her poem, "Three Moments," she wrote about a young girl who is unable to weep:

> *She cried: O mother, where are they,*
> *The tears that used to flow*
> *So easily? One single drop*
> *Might save my reason now, or stop*
> *My heart from breaking...*

The single outlet she allowed herself was verse. In her poem, "House to Home," she records the effect this experience had on her. She begins her use of winter images of cold, barren bleakness to describe the state of her inner world. This imagery would be a recurrent metaphor throughout her life:

That night destroyed me like an avalanche;
One night turned all my summer back to snow:
Next morning not a bird upon my branch,
Not a lamb woke below...

Already in delicate health, her heartbreak sent her into deeper decline. It sapped her creative energy. She wrote to William that the days were a blur, each resembling the other. Several months after their break-up, Christina fainted when she saw Collinson on the street. She wrote little at this time. What she did write was dark and despondent:

Song

When I am dead, my dearest,
    Sing no sad songs for me;
Plant thou no roses at my head,
    Nor shady cypress tree:
Be the green grass above me
    With showers and dewdrops wet:
And if thou wilt, remember,
    And if thou wilt, forget.

I shall not see the shadows,
    I shall not fear the rain;
I shall not hear the nightingale
    Sing on as if in pain:
And dreaming through the twilight
    That doth not rise nor set,
Haply I may remember,
    And haply may forget.

The following years were marked by loss and financial hardship. Gabriele Rossetti's health and eyesight failed, forcing him into retirement. This left the family in deep financial distress. Everyone tried to contribute to the family coffers, except for Dante Gabriel, of course. He continued his painting and asked for money. They moved to a smaller house. William took a second job. Mrs. Rossetti and her daughters turned to the only professions open to women in Victorian England. Maria found a position as a governess, and Christina helped her mother open a day school.

Unfortunately, London was full of schools run by penurious women. The Rossetti's were not able to attract enough students. In addition, Christina did not enjoy teaching though she loved children. She missed the intellectual stimulation of her brothers and literary friends. They closed down their school after two years, adding another parallel with the Brontës' who hoped to sustain themselves by establishing a school for girls in Yorkshire.

Life was changing. The P.R.B. was fracturing. Dante Gabriel wrote to Christina, *"So now the whole Round Table is dissolved."* Both of her Polidori grandparents died in the same year. When Christina learned of the death of her venerable old grandfather, she collapsed and cried, *"Oh my dear grandfather! Oh my dear grandfather!"*

The Rossetti's came into a small inheritance with the death of the elder Polidori's. It was not a large sum, but coupled with William's income, it would guarantee them a comfortable existence without the strain of having to find extra income to survive. William rented the family a larger home in the Regents Park neighborhood near their old church. This was a happy move; however, it was too taxing on Christina's father, Gabriele. Already in ill health, he began to weaken quickly. The family kept a death watch with him for several days. A former Dante student of Gabriele's, Charles Cayley, called on his old teacher twice during the last days. Christina was particularly endeared to him when he kept watch with the family until the end by respectfully waiting in a downstairs room.

Gabriele Rossetti passed away on April 26, 1854, just four months after grandfather Polidori died. This was the third death in the family in the space of one year. He left everything to his wife, Frances, and was buried at Highgate Cemetery. When she recovered from the initial shock of her husband's death, Frances did something shocking that belied her excessive religious fanaticism. She burned all surviving copies of a book he had written that she considered to be irreligious and dangerous.

With the stress of financial worries gone and the family back together under one roof, Christina entered a happy time of creative flow. Between the years 1854 and 1862, she wrote her best poetry. In August 1854, she wrote to the editor of "Blackwood's Magazine:"

> "...poetry is with me, not a mechanism, but an impulse and a reality; ... I know my aims in writing to be pure and directed to that which is true and right."

She was in full command of her poetic gifts now. She experimented with metrical innovations and rhyming variations. She joined Emily Dickinson and Elizabeth Barrett Browning in using half rhyme—pairing *pure* with *store*, *heaven* with *even*, and *blossom* with *bosom*. This was not widely accepted at the time. Many even felt the use of half rhyme ruined the poetry. She also developed her own poetic devices. One of the most unique was the use of a conversational pattern of question/answer. *"Who has seen the wind? Neither I nor you."* She had a lovely way of lyrically using word repetition for emphasis — *"deep beyond deep"* and *"snow on snow"*.

Dante Gabriel was creatively flourishing as well. He had found a new model, a Pre-Raphaelite ideal in Lizzie Siddal. He was captivated by her at first sight when he found her in her father's cutlery shop. Only sixteen years old, she was tall, had a long neck, large agate eyes and angular features. Her crowning feature that nearly bewitched Dante Gabriel was her magnificent mane of reddish gold hair that fell in crimped waves to her waist. They began a strange svengali-like love affair, and he painted her obsessively for the next five years.

William was writing poetry and making a name for himself as an art and literary critic. He and Dante Gabriel hobnobbed with all the literary lions of London — Alfred Lord Tennyson, James McNeill Whistler, Algernon Charles Swinburne, Ford Madox Brown, Robert and Elizabeth Barrett Browning. William set up opportunities for Christina to meet many of her literary peers, but because of her shyness and wariness of self-promotion and vanity, she rarely made appearances. When family friend Reverend Charles Dodgson (who wrote "Alice in Wonderland" under the name Lewis Carroll) offered to show Christina and her mother the sights of Oxford, she thanked him for his offer but asked for pictures of Oxford instead. She wrote, *"…it is characteristic of us to miss opportunities. A year or two ago I had a chance of seeing Cambridge, and of course, missed it."*

The P.R.B. was enjoying a renaissance. Acclaimed author and philosopher, John Ruskin, had taken note of them and was writing articles in their favor. New members were joining the Brethren and their art was gaining a following. Dante Gabriel was making quite a bit of money selling his work; yet, he was chronically broke and always in debt to family and friends. Christina published three poems in "Macmillan's Magazine" in 1861, one of which received wide acclaim and remains one of her finest works. It is a lyrical parable in the form of a conversation about salvation. One's walk through life is represented as an ascent up a steep hill. Having faith in finding one's place of comfort in heaven is represented at the top of the hill by an inn:

Uphill

Does the road wind up-hill all the way?
Yes, to the very end.
Will the day's journey take the whole long day?
From morn to night, my friend.

But is there for the night a resting-place?
A roof for when the slow dark hours begin.
May not the darkness hide it from my face?
You cannot miss that inn.

Shall I meet other wayfarers at night?
Those who have gone before.
Then must I knock, or call when just in sight?
They will not keep you standing at that door.

Shall I find comfort, travel-sore and weak?
Of labour you shall find the sum.
Will there be beds for me and all who seek?
Yea, beds for all who come.

In 1862, at age thirty-two, Christina published a poem that firmly established her as the leader of Pre-Raphaelite poetry—"Goblin Market." It is a mysterious and disturbing work that was illustrated by Dante Gabriel with images as haunting and emotional as the words. Christina always insisted that it was nothing more than a children's fairytale, but there is something far deeper in the text than a straightforward fable. Its narrative is underpinned with grotesque and erotic images that take the reader into a borderline region of subliminal messages that shift between the allegorical, the psychological and the religious.

The tale begins with two sisters, Laura and Lizzie, innocents who live in a safe and ordered world:

Golden head by golden head
Folded in each other's wings,
They lay down in their curtained bed...
Cheek to cheek and breast to breast
Lock'd together in one nest.

They are awakened by the call of goblin men enticing them to eat their fruits that are *"honey to the throat, But poison to the blood."* The description of the goblin fruit is an orgiastic feast of words:

> *Morning and evening*
> *Maids heard the goblins cry:*
> *'Come buy, come buy:*
> *Apples and quinces,*
> *Lemons and oranges,*
> *Plump unpecked cherries,*
> *Melons and raspberries,*
> *Bloom-down-cheeked peaches,*
> *Apricots, strawberries;*
> *All ripe together.*
> *Figs to fill your mouth,*
> *Citrons from the South,*
> *Sweet to tongue and sound to eye:*
> *Taste them and try*
> *Come buy, come buy.*

Lizzie admonishes Laura:

> *'We must not look at goblin men,*
> *We must not buy their fruits:*
> *Who knows upon what soil they fed*
> *Their hungry thirsty roots?'*

But Laura is attracted and intrigued:

> *'Look Lizzie, look, Lizzie,*
> *Down the glen tramp little men,*
> *One hauls a basket,*
> *One bears a plate,*
> *One lugs a golden dish*
> *Of many pounds weight.*

> *How fair the vine must grow*
> *Whose grapes are so luscious;*
> *How warm the wind must blow*
> *Through those fruit bushes…'*

Lizzie remains firm but Laura cannot resist:

> *"No," said Lizzie, "No, no, no;*
> *Their offers should not charm us,*
> *Their evil gifts would harm us."*
> *She thrust a dimpled finger*
> *In each ear, shut eyes and ran.*
> *Curious Laura chose to linger*
> *Wondering at each merchant man.*

The grotesque goblins have both human and animal features:

> *One had a cat's face,*
> *One whisked a tail,*
> *One tramped at a rat's pace*
> *One crawled like a snail,*
> *One like a wombat prowled obtuse and furry,*
> *One like a ratel tumbled hurry-skurry.*

Laura longs to taste the fruit, but she has no money. The goblins make a sly suggestion:

> *"You have much gold upon your head,"*
> *They answer'd all together:*
> *"Buy from us with a golden curl."*
> *She clipp'd a precious golden lock,*
> *She dropp'd a tear more rare than pearl,*
> *Then suck'd their fruit globes fair or red.*

Laura gorges herself on the goblin fare:

> *Sweeter than honey from the rock,*
> *She never tasted such before...*
> *Fruits which that unknown orchard bore;*
> *She sucked and sucked and sucked the more*
> *She sucked until her lips were sore;*
> *Then flung the emptied rinds away*
> *And knew not was it night or day...*
> *As she turned home alone...*

At first, Lizzie's hunger and curiosity is sated by her sensual feast, but she soon wants more. "*I ate and ate my fill, yet my mouth waters still.*" To her horror, she discovers that once she has eaten, she could no longer see or hear the little men or obtain more fruit.

> "*Day after day, night after night,*
> *Laura kept watch in vain.*
> *In sullen silence of exceeding pain.*"

She begins to waste away for want of more. Lizzie fears that Laura will die. She resolves to buy fruit from the goblin men for her sister's sake:

> *She put a silver penny in her purse,*
> *At twilight, halted by the brook:*
> *And for the first time in her life*
> *Began to listen and look.*

She hears the goblins and sees them reeling towards her in a chaotic pack:

> *Laugh'd every goblin*
> *When they spied her peeping;*
> *Came towards her hobbling,*

Flying, running, leaping,
Puffing and blowing,
Chuckling, clapping, crowing,
Clucking and gobbling,
Mopping and mowing

Lizzie stands firm, tosses them her penny and asks to buy their fruit. The goblins invite her to stay and eat with them. She refuses and asks for her penny back. The goblins violently attack her and Lizzie gladly gives herself as a sacrifice:

Lashing their tails
They trod and hustled her,
Elbow'd and jostled her,
Claw'd with their nails,
Barking, mewing, hissing, mocking,
Tore her gown and soil'd her stocking,
Twitch'd her hair out by the roots,
Stamp'd upon her tender feet,
Held her hand and squeezed their fruits
Against her mouth to make her eat.

Lizzie utter'd not a word;
Would not open lip from lip
Lest they should cram a mouthful in
But laugh'd in heart to feel the drip
Of juice that syrupp'd all her face,
And lodg'd in dimples of her chin,
And streak'd her neck which quaked like curd.

Lizzie returns triumphantly to Laura, calling to her from the garden gate:

"Did you miss me?
Come and kiss me.
"Never mind my bruises,

> *Hug me, kiss me, suck my juices*
> *Squeezed from goblin fruit for you.*
> *Goblin pulp and goblin dew.*
> *Eat me, drink me, love me;*
> *Laura, make much of me;*
> *For your sake I have braved the glen*
> *And had to do with goblin merchant men."*

A cryptic scene ensues that can be interpreted as sensual or sacramental where Laura licks the juices from Lizzie's battered body:

> *She clung about her sister,*
> *Kiss'd and kiss'd and kiss'd her…*
> *Kiss'd her with a hungry mouth*

Laura recovers her health and senses. Praising the sister who saved her, she sings:

> *"For there is no friend like a sister*
> *In calm or stormy weather;*
> *To cheer one on the tedious way,*
> *To fetch one if one goes astray,*
> *To lift one if one totters down,*
> *To strengthen whilst one stands."*

A reading of "Goblin Market" leaves one feeling raw, uprooted, suspended between consciousness and subconsiousness, unsure of where to anchor. Its meaning is a slippery, shifting enigma. What is it? Is it a simple fantastical children's story, as Christina alleged? Is it a morality tale of temptation and sin? Is it a religious allegory of sacrifice and redemption? Is it an erotic account of sexual longing and appetite? Is it an exalted treatise on sisterly love? Is it a sophisticated interpretation of the human dilemma — a depiction of the unrelenting inner struggle between the conflicting sides of oneself—the side that longs to give in to passion and the side that struggles for control?

However one chooses to read it, "Goblin Market" is brilliant in its depth and breadth. It is a lyrical metaphor that taps a vast psychological landscape that touches the edges of divine symbolism and sensual carnality.

"Goblin Market" won immediate critical praise and public embrace. Copies of it quickly found their way to the United States before it was even published on the American continent. American readers, including Ralph Waldo Emerson, admired its religious connotations. Emily Dickinson, however, was seized by its magical qualities. She never commented directly upon Christina Rossetti or "Goblin Market," but images of goblins popped up in her work for the next several years.

It is not surprising that the years between 1861 and 1864 were the healthiest of Christina's life. She was enjoying recognition for her poetry, and she was falling in love. Her longtime friendship with Charles Bagot Cayley, the Italian student of her father's who had watched with the family at Gabriele Rossetti's death, was evolving into a warm romance. There was a marked upturn in the tone of Christina's letters at this time. She seemed so happy simply to love and be loved.

Charles Cayley was an Englishman of Russian descent who had the trust and respect of the entire Rossetti family. William wrote that Cayley *"belonged to a fine type of character... [which] a woman of an exceptional order might genuinely admire."* He had dark hair and dark, quiet eyes. His clothes were disheveled and ill-fitting *"yet with a kind of prim decorum."* He was awkward, academic and absent-minded. To Christina he was entirely endearing.

Charles and Christina readily connected on many levels. They both eschewed worldliness, preferring the sphere of the intellect. He did not seek to patronize or dominate her. They were both lovers of language, words and poetry. He respected her poetic gift. They both spoke Italian. Perhaps what sealed their bond was their shared sense of odd, intellectual humor which put them at ease with each other and provided fertile ground for intimacy to grow. They could plunge into the depths of slow, serious conversation and share laughter in the same minute. Christina wrote, *"The old feelings revive; Love whispers hope."*

After four years of very close friendship, Charles and Christina began to consider binding their lives together in marriage. However, the quandary of faith once again aborted her passions. Charles was an agnostic. He regarded religions as the same, *"a mixture of feeling with thought, assumption and legend, not with verification."*
After much contemplation, Christina decided that she could not achieve a complete union with him and abandoned, once and for all, the hope for intimate companionship in this life.

William was dismayed by Christina's refusal. Unable to imagine why Christina refused the love of one so well suited to her when she was in her late thirties, he surmised that money was the obstacle. He told them that he would offer any kind of support they needed. When Christina explained herself, William could neither understand nor sanction her decision. He urged her to change her mind and be happy with Charles. But

Christina, who had a force of will on any point of duty, remained immovable. William explained that:

> *"her love was as deep as it was often silent...Although she would not be his wife, no woman ever loved a man more deeply or more constantly."*

Of her character, he added:

> *"The narrow path was the only one for her, and a lion in the same path made no difference. Tenacity was the very essence of her being."*

Christina wrote a veiled account of her love story in a series of sonnets, similar to Elizabeth Barrett Browning's love story in her "Sonnets from the Portuguese." However, unlike Mrs. Browning's story of love fulfilled, Christina's sonnets tell a story of love renounced. In Sonnet No. 6 of *Monna Innominata*, Christina reveals the heart of her sacrifice:

> *Trust me, I have not earned your dear rebuke,*
> *I love, as you would have me, God the most;*
> *Would lose not Him, but you, must one be lost,*
> *Nor with Lot's wife cast back a faithless look*
> *Unready to forego what I forsook;*
> *This say I, having counted up the cost,*
> *This, tho' I be the feeblest of God's host,*
> *The sorriest sheep Christ shepherds with His crook.*
> *Yet while I love my God the most, I deem*
> *That I can never love you overmuch;*
> *I love Him more, so let me love you too;*
> *Yea, as I apprehend it, love is such*
> *I cannot love you if I love not Him.*
> *I cannot love Him if I love not you.*

Charles accepted Christina's decision with the quiet dignity and grace that she so admired in him. Neither she nor Charles ever married. They remained constant and dear friends for the rest of their lives. In 1867, he sent her a poem of wishing and reminiscence:

> *Methought we met again like parted mates in a bower,*
> *And from between our hearts a sword was lifted…*
> *And long we talked of mysteries*
> *And no laws o' the world or flesh presumed any longer*
> *To sunder or mingle us…*

Years later, Christina wrote a letter to Charles that hinted at regret:

> *"…very likely there was a moment when – and no wonder – those who loved you best thought very severely of me, and indeed I deserved severity at my own hands,--I never seemed to get much at yours."*

After Christina relinquished her final hope for love in this life, she determined that her calling was to be a companion to her aging mother, a writer of poetry and a supplicant to her God. Christina's life became one of *"self-postponement"* and *"hope deferred."* Her poetry became increasingly melancholy. It was marked by a constant theme of longing unfulfilled – longing for lost love, longing for children she would never have, longing for union with the God she adored, and longing to be done with her life of loneliness and pain:

> *I wish I were dead, my foe,*
>   *My friend, I wish I were dead,*
> *With stone at my tired feet*
>   *And a stone at my tired head.*

In her poem, "An Immurata Sister," she wastes not a word in describing her sense of inner imprisonment and yearning to be free. Her Latinized use of the word, "immure," in the title – which means to enclose within walls, to be entombed – perfectly captures her sense of entrapment:

An Immurata Sister

Men work and think, but women feel;
And so (for I'm a woman, I)
And so I should be glad to die,
And cease from impotence of zeal,
And cease from hope, and cease from dread,
And cease from yearnings without gain,
And cease from all this world of pain,
And be at peace among the dead.

Christina renounced the world and focused her affections on the only Man who could provide her with the transcendent love she craved – Jesus Christ. Her writing became primarily devotional. The tenderest devotions to God mingled with her poetic lamentations of lost love. An oft revisited theme is the difference between divine love and human love – one transient and corruptible, the other faultless and eternal:

The Heart Knoweth Its Own Bitterness

I long to pour myself, my soul,
Not to keep back or count or leave
Were I to pour you could not hold
I long for one to stir my deep –
I have had enough of help and gift –
I long for one to search and sift
Myself, to take myself and keep.

God's Singers

> *Not in this world of hope deferred,*
> *This world of perishable stuff;--*
> *Here moans the separating sea,*
> *Here harvests fail, here breaks the heart;*
> *There God shall join and no man part,*
> *I full of Christ and Christ of me.*

As she reconciled herself to the reality of her life, she wrote of her *"oceanic feelings"* of worldly despair that were mercifully lifted by moments of heavenly comfort. Throughout the years, her poetry became a unique weave of loneliness and faithfulness:

A Better Resurrection

I have no wit, no words, no tears;
  My heart within me like a stone
Is numbed too much for hopes or fears;
  Look right, look left, I dwell alone;
I lift mine eyes, but dimmed with grief
  No everlasting hills I see;
My life is in the falling leaf:
  O Jesus, quicken me.

My life is like a faded leaf,
  My harvest dwindled to a husk;
Truly my life is void and brief
  And tedious in the barren dusk;
My life is like a frozen thing,
  No bud nor greenness can I see:
Yet rise it shall — the sap of Spring;
  O Jesus, rise in me.

My life is like a broken bowl,
   A broken bowl that cannot hold
One drop of water for my soul
   Or cordial in the searching cold;
Cast in the fire the perished thing,
   Melt and remould it, till it be
A royal cup for Him my King:
   O Jesus, drink of me.

Christina had always disregarded fashion, a trait she shared with Emily Brontë and Emily Dickinson. Women's fashion in the nineteenth century was highly ornamental and restrictive. Ignoring fashion was a statement of separateness and difference. But now her appearance and manner of dress became more severe, another facet of her self-denial. Author and literary critic Sir Edmund Gosse wrote:

> *"Her dark hair was streaked across her olive forehead, and turned up in a chignon; the high stiff dress ended in a hard collar and plain brooch, the extraordinarily ordinary skirt sunk over a belated crinoline, and these were inflictions hard to bear from the High-Priestess of Pre-Raphaelitism."*

Dante Gabriel could not agree more. He had once flippantly told her (in a way that only a brother could tell a sister,) *"Well, Christina, your heart may be like a singing bird, but you dress like a pew-opener."*

Christina's health declined with her happiness. She had frequent headaches. Her hands began to shake, making it difficult to write. A swelling in her throat made it difficult to swallow. She was diagnosed with an overactive thyroid, or Graves' disease.

It marred her looks by causing an abnormal protrusion of the eyeballs. Her skin darkened; her hair fell out. William said she looked a *"total wreck."* Her self-restraint was tried. William wrote that she seemed *"more scared and upset than I think I ever before saw her at any moment of pain or distress."* Her modesty was tried. Very conscious of her deteriorating looks, which she called *"habitual ugliness,"* she would see no one outside the family except Charles Cayley.

Time was also taking its toll on Dante Gabriel. His impetuous lifestyle was catching up with him. After years of resistance, he finally married Lizzie Siddal out of a sense of obligation. It was a disastrous marriage. Gabriel felt trapped and continued affairs with other women. Lizzie, ever unsure of herself and where she stood with Dante Gabriel, became a drug addict. After giving birth to a stillborn child, she committed suicide. Dante Gabriel was haunted by guilt and began a steady descent into alcoholism and drug addiction and began developing mental illness.

It was a difficult time for the Rossetti family. In addition to Dante Gabriel's collapse, Christina's crisis of health and an aging mother, Maria was struggling with cancer. William keenly felt the weight of responsibility for his family and was near a breakdown himself. But his somber mood was lifted when he became engaged to Lucy Madox Brown. It was a perfect match. Lucy, at thirty, was quite a bit younger than William, forty-four.

She was the daughter of Ford Madox Brown, long time family friend, painter and ally of the Pre-Raphaelites. She was a painter and, like William, an agnostic.

The Rossetti family was thrilled with the match. They had been close to the Brown family for years and had watched Lucy grow up. However, bringing a wife into the family home would have dramatic implications. Mrs. Rossetti had always been the strict and efficient matriarch of the family. For Christina, home had been a safe haven from the world, and many responsibilities were being passed to her as her mother aged. When Lucy entered the home, the balance of power would be capsized. The Rossetti house would have a new mistress.

Maria used this change as the impetus to fulfill her long time dream of entering the convent. She had long associated herself with the All Saints Community as an Outer Sister. In 1873, she disappeared into the convent completely and became an Anglican nun at age forty-six. Maria was elated. She told William that one of her main purposes for entering the Sisterhood was to *"obtain from God the grace of conversion for her brothers."* Dante Gabriel was not appreciative. He wrote that now his sister was to become *"one of those old things whom you see going about in a sort of coal-scuttle and umbrella costume."*

When William brought Lucy home, there was a good deal of tension between her and Christina. Neither woman felt like she had a place of her own. Christina and her mother started spending weeks at a time with the old aunts, Eliza and Charlotte Polidori. After Lucy gave birth to her first child, the family decided to make the arrangement permanent. The four women rented a home together at Torrington Square in London.

God's Singers

Christina wrote to Lucy, "*I hope when two roofs shelter us...that we regain some of the liking which we had as friends...now that we are sisters.*" Christina would live there for the rest of her life. Living with three old women, she began to call herself old as well, even though she was only in her mid-forties.

Meanwhile, Maria's condition worsened. She was well cared for by the nuns, and she approached death with joyful certainty about her salvation. She passed peacefully on November 24, 1876, at the age of forty-nine, just three years after she entered the convent. Instead of being buried at Highgate in the family plot, she was buried at the convent plot in Brompton. She did not want a sad funeral, and Christina and her mother did their best to honor her wishes. Christina wrote of the graveside service, "*...the sun made a miniature rainbow in my eyelashes.*"

Life for Christina and her three elderly women at Torrington Square was circumscribed. Christina rose at seven each morning and attended morning church services. When she returned home, she wrote letters and worked on her poetry and prose. Prose did not spring as spontaneously from her as poetry. She wrote, "*I work at prose and help myself forward with a little bits of verse.*" She spent her afternoons tending to the needs of the household and the old ladies—justifying family accounts, directing servants, doing laundry and making tea. In the evenings, she would read. Visitors to the house remarked on its absolute silence. One can imagine the swishing of skirts, the clink of teacups and the turning of pages breaking the quiescence. An evening visit from Charles Cayley for a game of whist was the highlight of a day. With his quiet propriety and dry humor, he was the perfect company for a house of aging matrons. The four women would generally go to bed early after an evening devotional and prayers.

She had twice postponed her life for the Lord, and duty would not let her leave her mother and aunts to take the veil as her sister had. She believed that her life was to toil so that others may live. She wrote to a friend:

> *"I do revere those exaltedly pious persons...who are fit for the monastic life: only I do not myself lay claim to such a gift...I have had a tiring day, and now I hear an arrival of clean clothes from the wash clamouring for me to look through them. So my **poet steps** must trudge upstairs to the humble work."*

We glimpse her daily routine of service and devotion in this prayer-poem:

> *My life is but a working-day,*
>   *Whose tasks are set aright:*
> *A while to work, a while to pray,*
>   *And then a quiet night.*
>
> *And then, please God, a quiet night.*
>   *Where Saints and Angels walk in white.*
> *One dreamless sleep from work and sorrow.*
>   *But reawakening on the morrow.*

William wrote that she lived, *"... a life which did not consist of incidents: in few things, external; in all its deeper currents, internal."*

Christina had been working on a collection of nursery rhymes. Her inspiration for them was memories of her own childhood. As William and Lucy grew their family, the addition of children to the Rossetti clan created more points of conflict for the sisters-in-law. Christina loved her nieces and nephews and even called William and Lucy's children *"My children, I may almost say, as none other can be so near to me."* However, children never come without noise and mess. Visits from William's brood not only disrupted Christina's contemplation, they ruffled her papers. There was also the problem of baptism. William and Lucy's agnosticism prevented them from baptizing their babies. This caused a great deal of concern to Christina and her mother.

One would never guess from reading <u>Sing-Song, A Nursery Rhyme Book</u>, published in 1872, that it was not written by the greatest mother and lover of children of all time. It was filled with the finest children's poetry of the nineteenth century. Nursery rhymes are written to be read aloud to children, and Christina's lyrical verses are delightful as they roll off the tongue:

> *My baby has a mottled fist,*
>   *My baby has a neck in creases;*
> *My baby kisses and is kissed,*
>   *For he's the very thing for kisses.*

Christina also employs her lovely question/answer technique to both teach and delight:

> *What are heavy? Sea sand and sorrow:*
> *What are brief? Today and tomorrow:*
> *What are frail? Spring blossoms and youth;*
> *What are deep? The ocean and truth.*

Christina's reputation continued to spread. Some even called her the finest woman poet of the English language. When author and editor, Mr. Patchett Martin, wrote an article declaring Christina to be a *"greater literary artist"* than Elizabeth Barrett Browning, Christina sent in a rebuttal. With typical self-effacement she wrote, "*I doubt whether the woman is born, or for many a long day, if ever, will be born, who will balance, not to say outweigh Mrs Browning.*"

Dante Gabriel's condition was growing much worse. He was in constant physical pain and partially paralyzed on one side of his body. He was tormented by past actions — his treatment of his father, of Lizzie Siddal and of his mistresses. He could not sleep without nightmares. He was delusional and paranoid and isolated himself from his friends. To get relief, he was mixing chloral hydrate — a hypnotic sedative, morphine and alcohol. Wracked by a disproportionate sense of guilt, he considered going to confession.

Like Emily Brontë was to Branwell, Christina was able to love and sympathize with Dante Gabriel without judging him. She may have chosen a very different path than her brother; nevertheless, she understood the destructive nature of his passion and his burden of guilt. She sympathetically encouraged him:

> "*...you are continually in my thoughts and always in my heart. I want to assure you that, however harassed by memory or by anxiety you may be, I have (more or less) ...gone through the same ordeal. I have borne myself until I became unbearable to myself, and then I have found help in confession and absolution and spiritual counsel and relief inexpressible...Don't think me merely as the younger sister whose glaring faults are known to you, but as a devoted friend also.*"

By the end of March 1882, Dante had deteriorated to a *"pitiable state."* A doctor diagnosed him with kidney failure as a result of long term chloral abuse. Christina and her mother traveled to Birchington-On-Sea, where he had gone for a change of air, to tend to him. When she arrived, Dante Gabriel's condition was even more dire than she had anticipated. She urgently summoned William to come, *"do not doubt the reality of poor dear Gabriel's illness."* Christina kept vigil with him throughout the nights. One of the last things Gabriel said was, *"It is beautiful, the world, and life itself. I am glad I have lived."* On Easter Day, April 9, Christina had just applied a poultice to him and his mother was rubbing his back, when he sat up suddenly, cried out twice, fell back on his bed, and died. It was two months before his fifty-fourth birthday.

The art community felt as though a light had gone out in their world. Even old friends with whom he had been estranged, like Holman Hunt, said, *"I feel like a part of my own life taken away."* Ford Madox Brown, one of Dante Gabriel's first painting teachers and Lucy Rossetti's father wrote:

> *"...there is no doubt poor dear Gabriel's life has been consumed the more rapidly owing to the continual outpouring of that poetry and picture which he seems to have been sent into the world to produce."*

Christina simply said that her brother Dante Gabriel was *"not only much beloved but truly lovable."*

The following year, 1883, William's baby son, Michael, who was not quite two years old, became suddenly ill. As the baby neared his end, Christina became tense and emotional about the state of the baby's soul. She implored William to allow her to baptize him. After discussing the matter, William and Lucy consented, reasoning that it would cause no harm to the child and would greatly ease Christina's mind. She performed the sacred rite unwitnessed. William recalled, *"I doubt whether an act of her life yielded her more heartfelt satisfaction."* They buried the baby in the family plot at Highgate.

A month after little Michael Rossetti died, Charles Cayley felt moved to put his affairs in order. He wrote to Christina, his dearest friend and the love of his life, asking if she would be the executrix of his small literary estate. Christina had already contemplated the moment when death would separate them:

> *When the time comes for us to part,*
> *And each of us must go our separate way,*
> *The moment which must come, the last moment*
>   *Whenever it may.*
>
> *When one of us must tread an unfamiliar path,*
> *The other following his usual course,*
> *Let no reproach suffuse our faces,*
>   *Let there be no remorse.*
>
> *If you go first, alone and strong*
> *Or if I go before you on the path,*
> *Let us remember everything we said:*
>   *That it was always Truth.*
>
> *How much I love you. Oh, how much!*
> *And could not show you what was in my heart,*
> *More, so much more than I could tell you*
>   *I loved with all my heart.*

Shortly thereafter, John Ingram asked Christina to author the life of Elizabeth Barrett Browning for his *Eminent Women* series. She replied that she would:

> "...write with enthusiasm of that great poetess...whom I was never so fortunate as to meet. But it would be necessary for me to know what would be Mr Browning's wish in the matter... having long enjoyed a slight degree of acquaintance with him I could not but defer to his wish."

Robert Browning was reluctant to make details of his wife's private life made known; so Christina refused the project.

Christina and her mother spent that summer at Birchington-On-Sea. She enjoyed seaside walks and reading the poetry of Emily Dickinson and Emily Brontë, both of whom had passed away. The *Memoir of Emily Brontë* was part of Ingram's series. Christina admired Emily's *"songs of defiance and mourning,"* but found the biography wanting for more details of the withdrawn poetess of the north. Of Emily Dickinson, Christina said that she had a gift but *"a startling recklessness of poetic ways and means."* One day on her walk to the sea, Christina brought herself to walk past the cottage where Dante Gabriel died. It had been renamed "Rossetti Bungalow."

1882 ended as it began—with a death. Charles Cayley's premonition was brought to pass. He died in his sleep December 6, the day after Christina's fifty-third birthday. He left Christina his writing desk. In it was a small envelope, containing a letter from her with a ring, and a large packet with the rest of her letters. Charles' sister Sophie wrote to her with characteristic Victorian discretion, *"you were I know the friend he valued most."* Was this a returned engagement ring? We will never know. Christina destroyed every letter. But she did, as always, leave us a hint in her verses:

> *Cold as the cold Decembers,*
> *Past as the days that set,*
> *While only one remembers*
> *And all the rest forget,-*
> *But one remembers yet.*

In the following years, the three elderly women with whom Christina lived became increasingly decrepit and dependent. By 1885, she wrote to a friend that their house had become a hospital. Aunt Charlotte was bedridden and required full time care. Aunt Eliza was physically stronger, but she was suffering the onset of dementia.

Frances Rossetti was over eighty years old and growing more enfeebled. Christina faced the inevitability that she would soon lose her beloved mother — the woman whose calmness, strength and piety she had spent her life emulating. Yet, always finding herself lacking, she made up for her deficiencies in devotion. They had hardly been apart a day in their lives. At age forty-eight, Christina wrote of her mother:

> *Blessed Dear and Heart's Delight,*
> *Companion, Friend and Mother mine,*
> *Round whom my fears and love entwine...*
> *My pleasure and my treasure*
> *O blessed Mother mine.*

Many have speculated that Christina's idolization of her mother went far beyond normal and that she may have lived a much freer and happier life if her mother had not maintained such an unyielding hold on her. Time was now breaking that hold, physically if not emotionally. In April 1886, Mrs. Rossetti injured her back in a fall in her bedroom. She was put to bed, and a doctor was called, but she never recovered. She quickly deteriorated and expired within a week, almost four years to the day that Dante Gabriel had died. Christina documented the death:

> *"I Christina G. Rossetti, happy and unhappy daughter of so dear a saint, write the last words....on April 8 did my dearest mother cease from suffering. My beautiful mother looked beautiful after death, so contented....I had her dressed in the 'widow's cap' she has worn more than 30 years."*

Not surprisingly, she suffered a breakdown of her health that summer. The old symptoms of panic attacks, severe headaches and a sense of suffocation returned. Yet, she continued to conscientiously care for the old aunts. Where the force of love was less, her sense of duty surged. She cared for them with no less assiduity than she had her revered mother. She gave up all outside society — leaving home only to go to church for her communions, confessions, prayers and oblations.

Aunt Charlotte was confined to her bed another four years before she died in 1889. She left Christina two-thirds of her estate on the understanding that she would continue to make donations to preferred charities. Christina was sixty-two years old, and for the first time in her life, she had enough resources to live comfortably without having to depend upon William. She still had senile Aunt Eliza to attend. And another trial was looming.

She became aware that her general ill health was taking on a more specific nature. She did not divulge it to William until she had consulted two doctors, received a diagnosis and decided upon treatment. In May 1892, she wrote him, *"Something brooding in my health has reached a point demanding sharp treatment."* She had breast cancer and had decided to undergo a mastectomy. Anticipating public curiosity, she authorized William to be honest about her condition. She had also made another decision, *"We are keeping this anxiety from Aunt Eliza."* William wrote that *"she took the announcement most bravely."* Though he worried, *"I hope she will consent to take chloroform or some other anaesthetic, but don't feel wholly confident she will."*

Christina may have perfected the art of self-denial, but fortunately, she accepted ether for the mastectomy which was performed in her own home. William came to the house and sat with Aunt Eliza during the procedure, ensuring all appeared normal. William wrote, *"Christina has borne herself like a heroine in this matter."*

The following month he accompanied her and a nurse to Brighton to convalesce. Now Christina's only job was to relax! After so many years of service, she was not sure if she knew how! She wrote to her sister-in-law, Lucy:

> *"One of my 'occupations' is to lie down! Another is to write letters. Another is to go out in a chair. Shall I reckon breakfasting in bed as an occupation?"*

The doctor gave her a good prognosis for recovery, but Christina had her misgivings.

The following year, 1893, Aunt Eliza finally died. It was four years after Aunt Charlotte died. Now Christina was alone in the big house with its echoing halls. She considered moving to a smaller place, but her doctor advised her not to move in her condition.

Her writing life was still active. She published *The Face of the Deep*, a devotional book that had taken her seven years to write while she attended her aging mother and aunts. Her publisher released a book of devotional poems, *Verses*, which had appeared previously in other prose works. This volume included her most enduring and best loved Christmas poem, "In The Bleak Midwinter." It was her last publication. She wanted to dedicate the book to William, but he felt that it would be inappropriate in light of his agnosticism. She was also being considered for the post of Poet Laureate of England.

Her breast cancer returned in the autumn of 1893. Only palliatives could be applied while she awaited her end. She lingered another year, her body weakening and her mind darkening. As her death neared, she was troubled and agitated in spirit. She wrote to William, "*I wish you would sometimes pray for me that I may not, after having (in a sense) preached to others, be myself a castaway.*"

After a life of sacrifice and devotion, rather than being comforted by her faith, she was terrified that she was unworthy to meet God. William wrote that Christina, "*always distrusted herself. All her life she felt — or rather she exaggerated — her deficiencies or backslidings.*" By August she was unable to leave the house to attend church. Her pastor visited her at home twice a week to give her communion. It frustrated William that every time Reverend Gutch came:

> "...he took it upon himself to be austere where all the conditions of the case called on him to be solacing and soothing. I could not find that his advent ever left Christina cheered, but rather more cheerless."

Christina's nephew, Ford Madox Ford remarked, "It has always seemed to me to be a condemnation of Christianity that it should have let such a fate harass such a woman."

In September, William had a bed moved into the drawing room. Christina spent her last months there, greatly comforted that it was the bed in which her mother had died. The doctors prescribed opiates for her pain, which was worsening. This caused her to be delusional at times. William said:

> "...some of her utterances were deeply painful...The fires of hell seemed more realistic than the blessings of heaven." Once she cried out, "How dreadful to be eternally wicked! For in Hell you must be so eternally!"

Christina realized that her mind was being affected by the opiates. One day she asked William if the cat that sat on her bed was really there, or was it an hallucination. She was often lucid and spoke with William of childhood memories. She also spoke of Charles Cayley, more than once, confiding to William that she had loved him *"in terms of almost passionate intensity."*

God's Singers

In her last days she was too weak to communicate, but her lips were moving in constant prayer. In the early morning of December 29, 1894, *"she gave one last sigh and died."* She was sixty-four years old.

Christina Rossetti was buried on January 5, 1895. A light snow dusted the ground. In keeping with English custom, she was laid in the same grave as her mother and father at Highgate Cemetery in London. William inscribed the headstone with one of Christina's verses that he felt best described her life:

> *Give me the lowest place; or if for me*
>   *That lowest place too high, make one more low*
> *Where I may sit and see*
>   *My God and love Thee so.*

One who was present at her funeral on that wintry morning described how, at the close of the service, the sun broke through the clouds and sparkled onto the snow and a robin on a leafless bush close by burst into song:

> *I heard the songs of Paradise:*
>   *Each bird sat singing in his place;*
> *A tender song so full of grace*
>   *It soared like incense to the skies.*

Christina as a Poet

Christina Rossetti's life was one great paradox. She lived a quiet and reclusive life; yet, she hobnobbed with a multitude of the greatest minds of her day. Though her heart beat strong and deep with romantic love, she never married. Though she wrote for children, she never had any.

Though highly gifted, her modesty would not allow her to acknowledge her own genius. She believed that her brothers' work was far superior to her own because they were men. William said, *"in a roomful of mediocrities she consented to seem the most mediocre as the most modest of all."* She saw the source of her immortality not in her art but in her obedience to God.

Nevertheless, Christina Rossetti is considered by many to be the greatest female poet of the English language. Sir Edmund Gosse, contemporary writer, critic and librarian for the House of Lords Library, wrote that as a devotional poet, she *"has not her equal in the English language."* Sir Walter Raleigh said, *"I think she is the best poet alive."*

Two years after Christina's death, her brother William published another volume of her poetry, called <u>New Poems</u>, and penned a memoir of his famous sister. In it, he gives us a close look into Christina's character and psychology. He said that Christina had two motivations: religion and affection. As both motivations are affairs of the heart, she was a wholly heart-led person. What made her such a tortured soul was that she believed her innate yearnings were incompatible with her religious fervor. She always had to cut off one part of herself to allow the other to live, which never allowed her wholeness. Consistently required to choose her religious convictions over her emotional needs caused profound conflict. She paid a high earthly price for heavenly reward:

> *Oh foolishest fond folly of a heart*
> *Divided, neither here nor there at rest!*
> *That hankers after heaven, clings to earth;*
> *That neither here nor there knows thorough mirth,*
> *Half-choosing, wholly missing, the good part.*

Even as she strove to always choose the better part, she was never sure of herself. No matter how hard she tried, she struggled with self-doubt to her last breath. She was in a state of continual despondency. Add this to her various health problems, it is no wonder she yearned to rest in death. There was to be no resolution for her in this life. Poetry was the only place the polarities of her soul could join in sublime union. Her self-loathing and sense of entrapment are painfully clear in the following poem:

Who Shall Deliver Me?

> *God strengthen me to bear myself;*
> *That heaviest weight of all to bear,*
> *Inalienable weight of care.*
>
> *All others are outside myself;*
> *I lock my door and bar them out,*
> *The turmoil, tedium, gad-about.*

If I could once lay down myself,
And start self-purged upon the race
That all must run! Death runs apace.

If I could set aside myself,
And start with lightened heart upon
The road by all men overgone!

God harden me against myself,
This coward with pathetic voice
Who craves for ease, and rest, and joys:

Myself, arch-traitor to myself;
My hollowest friend, my deadliest foe,
My clog whatever road I go.

Yet One there is can curb myself,
Can roll the strangling load from me,
Break off the yoke and set me free.

Though renunciation and self-effacement are continuous themes in Christina's poetry, she still loved what she renounced. Author Mary Bradford Whiting wrote for the Centenary Commemoration of her birth in December, 1930:

> *"Three out of her four grandparents were Italian, and her nature was shot through with that fire of the south which flames up at the sight of beauty and the touch of joy. That her poems are too full of tears is a charge that has been brought against them: but her tears are not a winter rain, cold and cheerless; they are tears of April, with the warm sun shining through them. Wherever her pages are opened, the love of all things beautiful flashes out in some glowing line."*

Through her struggle, she left the world a gift of poetry that cuts to the very core of human experience. Her depiction of man's eternal struggle as an infinite, spiritual being yearning for connection with his Maker, yet bound to a finite physical existence, is without parallel.

She had the faculty of articulating depth of emotion and the most exalted of feelings and putting them together in an exquisite arrangement of rhythm and sound. Her poetry is perfectly lyrical, having a metrical cadence all its own. William said:

> "...her habits of composition were entirely of the casual and spontaneous kind, from her earliest to her latest years. If something came into her head which she found suggestive of verse, she put it into verse. It came to her very easily, without meditating a possible subject and without her making any great difference in the first from the latest form of the verses which embodied it."

She wrote fantasy, verse for children, love poetry and religious devotional poetry. Her religious poetry is particularly supreme — even visionary, yet never didactic or doctrinal.

None Other Lamb

None other Lamb, none other Name,
  None other Hope in heaven or earth or sea,
None other Hiding-place from guilt and shame,
  None beside Thee.

My faith burns low, my hope burns low
  Only my heart's desire cries out in me
By the deep thunder of its wants and woe
  Cries out to Thee.

Lord, Thou art Life tho' I be dead,
  Love's Fire Thou art, however cold I be:
Nor heaven have I, nor place to lay my head,
  Nor home, but Thee.

Paradise

Once in a dream I saw the flowers
    That bud and bloom in Paradise;
More fair they are than waking eyes
    Have seen in all this world of ours.
And faint the perfume-bearing rose,
    And faint the lily on its stem,
And faint the perfect violet
    Compared with them.

I heard the songs of Paradise:
    Each bird sat singing in his place;
A tender song so full of grace
    It soared like incense to the skies.
Each bird sat singing to his mate
    Soft cooing notes among the trees:
The nightingale herself were cold
    To such as these.

I saw the fourfold River flow,
    And deep it was, with golden sand;
It flowed between a mossy land
    Which murmured music grave and low.
It hath refreshment for all thirst,
    For fainting spirits strength and rest:
Earth holds not such a draught as this
    From east to west.

Christina Rossetti

The Tree of Life stood building there,
    Abundant with its twelvefold fruits;
Eternal sap sustains its roots,
    Its shadowing branches fill the air.
Its leaves are healing for the world,
    Its fruit the hungry world can feed,
Sweeter than honey to the taste
    And balm indeed.

I saw the gate called Beautiful;
    And looked, but scarce could look within;
I saw the golden streets begin,
    And outskirts of the glassy pool.
Oh harps, oh crowns of plenteous stars,
    O green palm branches many-leaved –
Eye hath not seen, nor ear hath heard,
    Nor heart conceived!

I hope to see these things again,
    But not as once in dreams by night;
To see them with my very sight,
    And touch and handle and attain:
To have all Heaven beneath my feet
    For narrow way that once they trod;
To have my part with all the saints,
    And with my God.

Finally, as recounted in the prelude, here is the poem that started it all for us, "In the Bleak Midwinter." This is her best loved, most enduring poem. It was first set to music by Gustav Holst, and then by Harold Darke. It can still often be found on Christmas cards and recordings. Christina begins by painting a piercing picture: the wind moans, earth is hard as iron, water like a stone. Her repetition of the word *"snow"* to create the mental image of the depth of winter chills the reader each time it is read. Next, she draws a simple scene of a small place of warmth amidst the dreary cold that is sufficient for the Lord of All. The spare references to *"hay"* and a *"breastful of milk"* bring us into the reality of the moment:

In The Bleak Mid-winter

In the bleak mid-winter
    Frosty wind made moan,
Earth stood hard as iron,
    Water like a stone;
Snow had fallen, snow on snow,
    Snow on snow,
In the bleak mid-winter
    Long ago.

Our God, Heaven cannot hold Him,
    Nor earth sustain;
Heaven and earth shall flee away
    When He comes to reign:
In the bleak mid-winter
    A stable-place sufficed
The Lord God Almighty
    Jesus Christ.

Enough for Him, whom cherubim
    Worship night and day,
A breastful of milk
    And a mangerful of hay;
Enough for Him, whom angels
    Fall down before,
The ox and ass and camel
    Which adore.

Christina Rossetti

Angels and archangels
      May have gathered there,
Cherubim and seraphim
      Thronged the air;
But only His mother
      In her maiden bliss
Worshipped the Beloved
      With a kiss.

What can I give Him,
      Poor as I am?
If I were a shepherd
      I would bring a lamb,
If I were a Wise Man
      I would do my part,--
Yet what I can I give Him,
      Give my heart.

In the last stanza, in characteristic manner, she cuts to the heart of the matter. Where does she fit in? What can she give? The answer is simple, her heart. Indeed, in life, as in the poem, that is what she brought the Babe, her Savior, again and again in her sixty-four years.

201

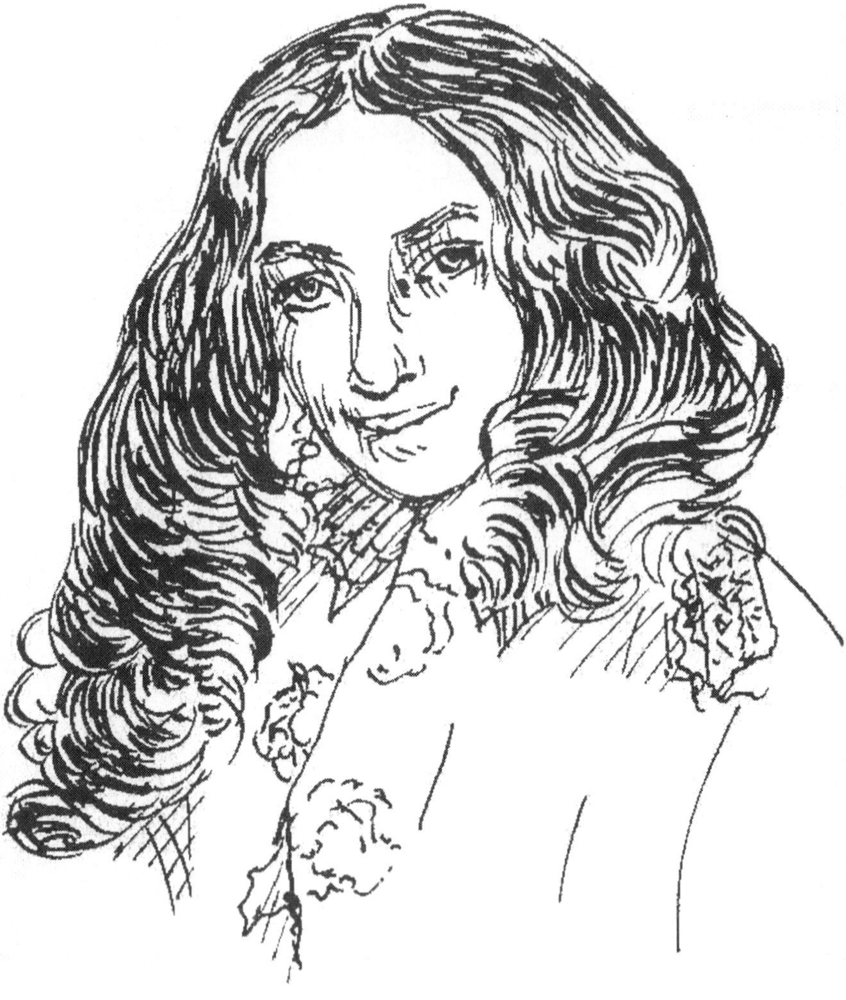

Elizabeth Barrett Browning
1806 – 1861

One cannot speak of Elizabeth Barrett without also speaking of Robert Browning. History has given them to us as a packaged pair for all *"love's eternity,"* to put it in Elizabeth's own words. When Robert, age thirty-three, first found Elizabeth, she was living in complete seclusion at the Barrett family home on Wimpole Street in London. She had not left her darkened room for nearly five years. The pallor of her skin was ashen; her eyes were like *"two dark caves."* The black silk dress she wore accentuated her alarming thinness and served to make her five foot one frame appear even more diminutive. Except for her thick glossy hair that hung round her face in large ringlets, she looked more ghost than human. Her nervous, thin, reedy voice revealed the whisper of the woman she had become. Her wraith-like appearance seemed wholly incongruous with her wild, passionate poetry.

She was thirty-nine years old and still under the complete control and domination of her iron fisted father, Edward Moulton-Barrett, as were the rest of her ten siblings. He ruled over his grown children like a monarch over his kingdom. He not only controlled their money and their comings and goings, he also attempted to control their thoughts and emotions by forbidding any of them to marry and *"break up the family."* He once made his daughter, Henrietta, drop to her knees and beg forgiveness for asking permission to have a suitor. She was approaching age forty at the time. Under this duress, only five of his eleven children ever married. When they did so, they were disinherited and never forgiven by their father.

Edward Moulton-Barrett began to build his familial *"empire"* in the West Indies where he lived as a teenager with the wealthy Clarke family after the death of his parents. He was innately shy to the point of being antisocial. Yet, at age eighteen, he secured a stake in the family fortune by marrying their twenty-four year old daughter, Mary Graham Clarke. Mary was not only Edward's thread to fortune and society, she was his only friend. They were married for twenty-seven years.

Elizabeth was their oldest child, and Edward absolutely idolized her. He affectionately called her Ba, establishing a family tradition of giving many of the children pet names. After Elizabeth, they had two more daughters, Arabel and Henrietta, and eight sons — twelve children in all. Eleven lived to maturity. Mary Barrett was forty-seven when she gave birth to her last child, Octavius. The sons were named:

- Edward – (Bro) his father's namesake
- Samuel – died in Jamaica at age twenty-eight
- Charles – (called Stormie because he was born during a violent thunderstorm); never married
- George – only son to become independent; a lawyer; never married
- Henry – married a woman named Amelia
- Alfred – married his cousin, Lizzie Barrett
- Septimus – (Settie)
- Octavius – (Occy) married a woman named Charlotte

Edward and Mary Barrett differed from other Victorian parents, offering books to their daughters as well as their sons. They acknowledged Elizabeth's intellectual and creative gifts early on and encouraged them. She had an insatiable appetite for learning. By the time she was ten years old, she had read Shakespeare, Pope's Homeric translations, Milton's _Paradise Lost_, and the histories of England, Greece and Rome. By the age of twelve she had written her own "*epic*" poem consisting of four books of rhyming couplets.

Elizabeth's passion for all things intellectual caused her to view her mother, who centered her life in husband and children, critically. It disgusted her, and she vowed not to repeat the drudgery she saw her mother endure. At age nine she announced to the family that she was dreadful at sewing, needle-work and other such female accomplishments and that poetry was her life's work. Her father responded to her declaration by dubbing her *"the poet laureate of Hope End"* and gave her a ten pound note — her first advance.

Elizabeth took the title seriously and flooded her family with ballads and odes commemorating various family holidays and events. With this early intellectual freedom, Elizabeth was an active, healthy child. However, like our other *singer's* families, there were limits to the Barretts' progressive parenting of their precocious daughter. That limit was adolescence. Until she was age twelve, Elizabeth had equal access to the family library and learned Greek alongside her brothers from the family tutor. At age thirteen, she learned the hard difference between girls and boys — school. Boys went to school and continued their learning, expanded their capabilities and life experiences. They saw new places, met new people and had a world of opportunity available them.

Girls stayed home. Elizabeth found out, just as all our singers did, that there was no place for her in a world dominated by men. There was only a place for her at home. It was as though the world kept moving and growing while she was cut off from it and left behind. Literally confined to Hope End, the family's five hundred acre estate, she was not allowed to leave without her father's permission, and he rarely gave it. She seldom saw anyone outside her family, and this frustrated her. With no place to go and no meaningful work to occupy her vivid imagination and boundless energy, she joined that band of creative Victorian women who struggled with depression and ill health throughout their adult lives.

From the onset of menstruation, upper and middle class Victorian women were regarded as *"delicate creatures."* Physical activity was discouraged; rest was encouraged. This prescribed inactivity produced weakness—for which the cure was more inactivity. A vicious cycle was set up for mass hypochondria, of which Elizabeth was a part. After a robust childhood, Elizabeth declared herself to be of *"natural ill health"* when she was thirteen years old. She felt weak, her heart raced, she swooned and fainted. Every ache and pain was magnified and analyzed.

A succession of doctors was called in to diagnose her varied, persistent symptoms. The treatments they prescribed were sometimes worse than the symptoms. Elizabeth endured slimy leeches, stinky poultices, cold showers and hot cupping (the placing of hot cups on the body to draw blood to the surface, leaving large cup shaped welts).

By the time she was sixteen, her doctor diagnosed her with early onset of a diseased spine. The diagnosis was made as a last resort, having not been able to find anything else wrong with her. He prescribed a change of climate, another typical medical treatment for Victorian women. Many believed that air had mysterious curative properties. Consequently, she was taken to a spa hotel where she spent one year strung up and suspended in a hammock-like contraption called a *"spine crib"* while waiting for the spine disease to *"show itself."*

It was while she was in this institution that she was first given opium, known as laudanum, to help her sleep. It was the Victorian equivalent of aspirin and was given as a general curative. The opium came in hard brown granules and was mixed in alcohol to make it palatable; so the actual doses that Elizabeth was taking is impossible to know. From then on, throughout her life, she was never without her laudanum. After one year, the spine disease never materialized. She was released from the spine crib physically weakened and addicted to opium. Her doctors sent her home with one last prescription: no intellectual activity. Excessive reading and writing were too exhausting for her debilitated constitution. She roundly rejected this prescription. Reading and writing is what made life worth living. She said:

> *"I suffer horribly when I don't read, the soul eats itself."*

Unable to escape the bitter lot of being a girl, she embraced the enforced seclusion that was the sentence of Victorian women and used it to fulfill her greatest passion: reading and writing. She ensured her solitude by nurturing her delicate constitution. She took a room at the top of the house, tucked away from the hustle and bustle of her large family, and called it her *"sanctum."* With her guarded peace, she relished in long lazy mornings reading and then spent her afternoons pouring her passions onto the page.

Poetry was *"real work at last."* She not only called herself a poet, she called herself *"one of God's singers."* However much she tried to convince herself that solitary study and writing was enough to fulfill her life, the true artist in her craved recognition. She nursed a nameless ambition, believing that she had something of worth to say to the world. What nobler calling could one have than to bring divine truth to the world through poetry?

Her brother, Edward, whom she affectionately called "Bro," became her conduit to the world. She insisted that he teach her everything he learned in school. And she, in turn, discussed her personal studies with him, which were remarkable. She read all the classics in their original languages of Greek and Latin. She learned Hebrew so that she could read the Old Testament, from beginning to end, in its original language. Their letters are an intellectual treasure trove containing lessons from Bro on hexameter verse to Elizabeth's analysis of Shelley's poem "Adonais."

Elizabeth not only devoured the classics, she kept up with current events by reading the newspaper every day. She voraciously read everything currently in print—literary magazines and that new, controversial literary genre, the novel. She began in earnest to seek publication for her own work. She sent Bro manuscripts regularly to be delivered to various London publishers. She felt that if she could catch the eye of other poets and have discourse with them, her limited life would have more meaning. By the time she was twenty-one, she had begun to publish successfully and generate a small income independent of her father. Like Emily Dickinson, she corresponded regularly with other literary figures of the times.

Now we see the pattern begin again—a creative woman physically confined by cultural boundaries coming to embrace her restrictions as a path to freedom. Over time, the culturally imposed seclusion becomes self-imposed and breeds an abnormal shyness. All the while she reaches intellectually beyond the boundaries for poetic union with the soul of the world.

The Barrett family life became more austere when her mother, Mary, died unexpectedly at age fifty-one. Her father was stricken; yet, ever the soul of propriety, he never lost control of his emotions. He instructed his children on grief, allowing them to weep, *"but within bounds."* Elizabeth recalled this time as *"one of unrelieved gloom."*

Elizabeth's shock at her mother's sudden death caused her to disconnect from all shows of grief. She was stilted, mute and emotionless even though she was surrounded by grieving, tears and heavy black mourning dress. Bro was alarmed by her odd behavior. But Elizabeth followed the example of the father she idolized. Rather than viewing his severity as odd, she perceived it as fortitude and self-control. She was inspired by it. Edward Barrett assuaged his loneliness by sleeping with Settie and Occy, who were four and six at the time. His religious fervor increased. He viewed the world as corrupt and was determined to keep his family pure and removed from it.

The next Barrett family setback was the loss of their West Indies sugar plantation fortune because of the abolition of slavery in the British Empire. They had to sell and leave their beloved estate, Hope End. Edward moved his family to Wimpole Street in London, an area popular with families from West Indies ties. However, the damp, dirty London air strained Elizabeth's weak lungs and she was prescribed a change of air again.

Following doctor's orders, she lived in the coastal village of Torquay, in Devonshire, to convalesce for three years. Elizabeth loved the coast and was enchanted by the sea. She said she was almost as fond of it as she was of poetry, saying; *"The sea is visible poetry."* But she was lonely and miserable without her family; so they came when they could to ease her homesickness. It was during one of these visits that she suffered the worst blow of her life.

At the end of one of his visits, Elizabeth begged her favorite brother, Bro, to stay longer with her. He agreed and a few days later went sailing on the sea with several friends. Their little boat was caught in a sudden squall, and all three of them drowned. She felt responsible for his death because she had encouraged him to stay. Stricken, she again went into a state of paralytic shock. She wrote that she *"... could speak not nor shed a tear but lay for weeks - and months - half-conscious, half-unconscious with a wandering mind."*

When she finally recovered enough to function again, she became irrationally fearful and morose. She was afraid to be happy. She wrote:

> *"There is no kind of enjoyment which one can have on this side of the grave without paying its price in pain."*

She feared that disaster and tragedy lurked around every corner. She was afraid to let any member of her family out of her sight. And she joined her father's zealous crusade to keep the family together at all costs. Her philosophy was to do nothing and go nowhere to ensure less chance of harm. She feared that if they were ever separated something else terrible might happen. She cried and was overwrought by nervousness whenever a family member had to be away from home.

Elizabeth wrote no letters to any of her correspondents for months. She finally took pen in trembling hand again and wrote of anguish to her friend and fellow author, Mary Mitford. Mrs. Mitford knew intuitively that she was beyond human comfort and offered to give Elizabeth her cocker spaniel's new puppy, Flush.

After several polite refusals, Elizabeth accepted Mrs. Mitford's gift, and one might say that her first great love affair began. Elizabeth was completely enamored with Flush. He never left her side, even sleeping in her bed. Grateful for the little dog that brought Elizabeth back to life, the whole family joined in pandering to Flush's every whim. He would not eat his daily bread unless it was liberally buttered, and he turned his nose up at mutton, preferring more expensive beef. He got a daily bath and had a special shawl that he liked to lie on near Elizabeth's fire.

Flush was also the subject of several little dramas. A London dognapper known as *"The Fancy"* stole Flush three times and held him for ransom. Elizabeth paid the ransom secretly each time so that her father would not find out.

Elizabeth also acquired another lifelong companion, a personal maid, who was twenty-four years old, named Elizabeth Wilson. Our poet simply called her Wilson. Wilson served Elizabeth faithfully until the end of her life, eventually following her mistress out of the country at great personal cost. Elizabeth was thirty-eight, and one year away from meeting Robert Browning. Wilson would be with the Browning's for fifty-eight years.

By 1844, Elizabeth was thirty-nine years old and had established a safe and tidy life for herself. She lived in a bubble within a bubble. The outer bubble was the large xenophobic Barrett family of adult children whose master was the autocratic "Papa" Barrett. The inner bubble was the enclosed world that Elizabeth created for herself. She again chose the furthermost room in the house as her "*sanctum,*" just as she had done at Hope End. It was a small, encapsulated realm unto itself. The room had a window, which did little good as it could not be opened and let in little natural light because of the overgrown ivy outside. Elizabeth used this warm, enclosed windowsill to hatch doves!

The room was furnished with a curtained bed, a fireplace, a couch and a writing desk. With her adored dog and her personal maid bringing all her meals to her, Elizabeth did not leave her room for five years! She lived by her own schedule—sleeping late, eating whenever she wanted, or not. Her delicate digestive system did not care much for food. She spent her time reading and writing for publication as well as maintaining her many correspondences with the outside world. The person dearest to her heart was her father, for whom her love bordered on worship. Papa came to her sanctum every evening for prayer.

Elizabeth yearned for human connection. Hers was a passionate nature. However, she had become phobic about meeting people face to face. Other than her family members, she let few into her sanctum. She had succeeded in living vicariously through her daily reading and correspondence. When she did see someone outside her family circle, her heart would race, her brow would bead with sweat and she had to be steadied by the hand of one of her dear sisters. The chosen few that she saw from time to time included Mrs. Mitford, her cousin John Kenyon, and Anne Thackeray Ritchie (daughter of William Makepeace Thackeray and another female author of the day).

Mrs. Mitford and Anne Thackeray Ritchie each left descriptions of Elizabeth. Mrs. Mitford wrote that Elizabeth had…

> "…*a slight, delicate figure, with a shower of dark curls falling on each side of a most expressive face; large, tender eyes, richly fringed by dark eyelashes, and a smile like a sunbeam.*" Anne described her as "*very small and brown with big, exotic eyes and an overgenerous mouth.*"

Though Elizabeth was contented with her limited existence, she harbored a secret fantasy. She wanted to see Italy. She confessed that her desire to see Italy made her *"sigh like a furnace."* It was into this hermetic life that the totally unexpected would occur—Robert Browning.

Elizabeth's friendship with Robert Browning began when she completed two volumes of poetry. She had hurriedly written a small poem to balance the length of her two volumes. It was called "Lady Geraldine's Courtship." In it, she paid passionate tribute to some fellow poets such as Wordsworth and Tennyson. The longest tribute was to Robert Browning, having admired his poetry for years. She specifically complimented his poem, "Paracelsus," from his recently completed work, "Bells and Pomegranates." In graceful and vivid language, she wrote:

> *"Or from Browning some pomegranate which, if cut deep down the middle, shows a heart within blood-tinctured of a veined humanity."*

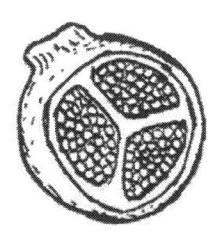

It was customary for Robert to respond. At the urging of his personal friend, who was Elizabeth's cousin, John Kenyon, he did so. Robert wrote and thanked her, thus ushering in one of the most dramatic romances of the nineteenth century. The confirmed bachelor of thirty-three years met the confirmed invalid of thirty-nine years. Sixteen months later neither was still such.

Robert wrote his first letter to Elizabeth in January 1845. He returned her compliment by expressing admiration for her writing:

> *"I cannot say or sing the pleasure your way of writing gives me. I love your verses with all my heart, dear Miss Barrett, I do, as I say, love these books with all my heart – and I love you too."*

Though Elizabeth often received admiring letters about her work, none of them were as open or passionate as Robert's.

Until this time, Papa Barrett had succeeded in keeping Elizabeth childlike in her knowledge and experience of men. She had had limited interchange with them except for her brothers. Her romantic and sexual feelings were as yet unawakened. Passion was a spiritual ideal for her. In a soulmate, she looked for one whose intellect and poetic passion could match her own.

When she received his letter, she felt that she had found her spiritual soulmate at last. She recognized in him a kindred spirit of passion and poetry that was in concert with her own heart. She was beside herself with joy and wrote back to Robert immediately, inviting him for poetic discussions and critique.

Three letters from him and three letters from her flew between them in the space of three weeks. They agreed to write to each other about their work — for comment, critique and encouragement. Elizabeth barraged him with questions. Which books had he read? What were his writing hours? Which poets did he admire most? How important was praise to him? Within a month they were sharing life stories and confidences.

Robert's admiration and desire to meet her increased with every letter. He naturally assumed that their letters were a precursor to a meeting. He knew she was an invalid, but he did not yet know the extreme nature of her reclusiveness.

Elizabeth feared meeting Robert. She worried that her person would not hold the same attraction for him as her writing. She was afraid that if they met, it would spoil their relationship. She used her invalid status to delay their meeting. She told him that she would feel stronger if she waited until spring to meet him. But when spring came, she was still avoiding their meeting.

Robert's feelings were hurt. Did she not know him better than that? Did she distrust him? Realizing that this issue was turning into an obstacle, Elizabeth reluctantly agreed to meet. After four months of correspondence, they made an appointment to meet — the following Tuesday, May 20, at two in the afternoon. The meeting was arranged at a time when Papa was out of the house.

Elizabeth lay on her couch filled with dread as the two o'clock hour approached. Her heart nearly stopped when she finally heard his footfall on the stair outside her door. But the moment he entered the room, her panic subsided. She felt an instant connection with him. By the time he left an hour later, she had discovered a passion she had never felt before. She wrote to him, *"When you came, you never went away."*

The man that Elizabeth met had had a swarthy complexion with *"hair as black as a raven's wing and as coarse as a horse's tail."* His head was large for his five foot six frame. His face was handsome and polished.

Robert came from a family whose sociability was the exact opposite of Elizabeth's. He never worried whether or not he would have something to say in another's company. There was always so much to say.

From that day forward, Robert and Elizabeth wrote to each other nearly every day and he visited her, secretly, at two p.m. every Tuesday for one hour. Of his love for her and their precious meetings, Robert wrote:

> *"I love you because I **love** you; I see you 'once a week' because I cannot see you all day long; I think of you all day long, because I most certainly could not think of you an hour less, if I tried."*

Robert and Elizabeth's letters, all five hundred seventy four of them, have been published and have become part of the literary canon that they have left behind. They are the most remarkable correspondences of their kind. They were quite open and uninhibited for having been written in the Victorian Age. Perhaps it is because they were both inexperienced in courting. Their romance was fired by the fervency of first love. They embraced each other fearlessly and without reservation. Elizabeth had never felt so understood, so at ease with another human being. It was as though they had discovered the true mating of a man and a woman — the marriage of minds.

They stimulated each other intellectually and enjoyed critiquing each other's work. An anecdotal story of their dynamic comes to us from the play, "The Barretts of Wimpole Street." When Robert struggles to explain a passage to Elizabeth from his volume, "Sordello," he says:

> *"Well, Miss Barrett, when that passage was written, only God and Robert Browning understood it. Now, only God understands it."*

Even when they disagreed on a subject, which was not often, Elizabeth was deeply gratified to discover that Robert never flaunted the least bit of masculine superiority over her. She told him that she was pleased not to find in him any *"of the common rampant man-vices which tread down a woman's peace."* Rather, each insisted that the other was superior. They were endlessly deferential to each other, like two people waiting to go through a door and each saying to the other, *"After you." "No, after you."* Robert often said of Elizabeth, *"She is the genius. I am the clever person."*

Happiness was the best remedy for Elizabeth's health. She wrote to Mrs. Mitford:

> *"…it is miraculous, the feeling of sprouting life in me and out of me – and now I begin to sleep and to look altogether like another person."*

Life ceased to be so fearful and morose. She felt so renewed that she ventured out of her room for the first time in five years. She not only emerged from her room to sit in the sun, but she began taking short outings to Regents Park, at first pushed in a wheelchair by her maid, Wilson. Before long, Elizabeth was taking walks on her own. She even accepted a long standing invitation to visit her cousin, John Kenyon, at his home. As wonderful as these changes were, nothing could dissuade her from giving up her laudanum.

After the happiest and healthiest spring and summer of her life, Robert was concerned that another damp

English winter would end Elizabeth's newfound wellness. He encouraged her to go abroad to a warmer climate, such as Malta, for the season. However, Elizabeth was still horrified at the thought of breaking up her father's home even for a season. She tearfully recounted Bro's death to Robert. He assured her that she had made that vow under feelings of false guilt.

Robert requested a meeting with Mr. Barrett to declare his love for his daughter and express his concerns for her health. But the thought of the two of them meeting terrified Elizabeth, and she did everything in her power to ensure that it would not happen. She loved her father, but she feared him. Her love for Robert was wholly different. *"To love and be loved by Robert was to be free, happy and at ease. To love and be loved by her father was to feel anxious, constrained and afraid of offending."* Robert was redefining her concept of love.

Her father had loved and protected her, just as she had wanted him to do. He had put her on a pedestal, and until now she had enjoyed being there above everyone else. She had been unknowingly complicit in her own captivity. Now she wanted to get off the pedestal, but she did not know how. Papa welcomed Elizabeth's return to health and happiness. However, he regarded this change with a fear that quickly translated to rage. The stronger she became, the less dependent she was on him. He vigorously resisted losing control of his favorite child.

She gathered her courage and consented to broach the subject of going to Italy with her father. He strongly objected, saying that her health had improved enough without having gone to a warmer climate. He viewed her desire for this trip as a break in their relationship.

She viewed his refusal of the trip as a fault line in the bulwark of his love for her.

Of the rift between her and Papa, she wrote:

> *"The bitterest 'fact' of all is, that I had believed Papa to have loved me more than he obviously does... he would rather see me dead at his foot than to yield the point: (of going to Italy)... he is the victim. He isolates himself-and now and then he feels it, the cold dead silence all around... If he were not stronger than most men, he could not bear it as he does. Tyranny? Perhaps. Yet in that strange, stern nature, there is a capacity to love- and I love him- and I shall suffer, in causing him to suffer."*

Robert and Elizabeth had been exchanging letters for one year now. The poetical critique with which they began was now missing from their missives. They wrote only of the love they felt for each other from the *"deepest parts"* of their beings. They held nothing back. Robert wrote:

> *"All words are foolish – but I kiss your feet and offer you my heart and soul, dearest, dearest Ba."*

She answered:

> *"I am glad now, yes glad – as we were to have a miracle – to have it **so**, a born-miracle from the beginning... Dearest and most generous. No man was ever like you, I know! For my life, it is yours, as this year has been yours."*

As their second winter of clandestine meetings and penned passions turned into spring, the secrecy of their courtship began to wear on Robert. All their letter writing became detestable to him. He could no longer exist on letters and one scant hour with her each week. It was torment. He wrote:

> "I do hate, **hate** having to write and not kiss my answer on your mouth."

He wanted to approach Mr. Barrett, man to man, and ask for Elizabeth's hand in marriage. She agreed with him that:

> "The sense of mask-wearing for another year would be suffocating."

However, she could not overcome her fear of being honest with her father or shaming him and the Barrett family with an elopement.

Elizabeth and Robert argued for the first time—about how to marry, and when, whom to tell, and what to do about money. Neither of them had ever earned their own keep. Robert's marriage to Elizabeth would bring him recognition, as her fame as a poet preceded his. She also had more money than he from an inheritance from her grandfather. The idea of Elizabeth supporting them was a question of honor for Robert. Though it was distasteful to Elizabeth, he insisted on documents being drawn up stating that all that was hers would go to any children they may have and then to her sisters. They settled on a plan and date after six months of lively exchange. They were risking all they knew and had on each other.

The last letters they ever wrote to one another planned their departure. Robert would arrange for a marriage license and a cleric to marry them. Elizabeth would feign a visit to a friend, but would meet Robert at Marylebone Church instead. He wrote to her:

"Depend on me."

She promised him:

"I shall not fail you…I will not."

The night before their secret wedding, she took Wilson into her confidence and asked for her help. Wilson quickly agreed. She had already been indispensible to them during their courtship. It was she who had been faithful in posting and collecting certain letters. It was she who had deflected other visitors while a certain gentleman was with her mistress. Wilson's risk was just as great as Robert and Elizabeth's. If she were found out, she would certainly be immediately dismissed and denied reference for any future employment.

On Saturday, September 12, 1846, Elizabeth and Wilson left the house at eleven a.m. on pretense of taking a walk in the morning sun. They walked two hundred yards up Wimpole Street; then they turned the corner towards Marylebone Church where Robert was waiting for her with a ring in his pocket. His cousin, James Silverthorne, was with him. Elizabeth began to shake on the way and nearly fainted. Wilson steadied her and led her into a chemist's shop to purchase some smelling salts.

The sight of Robert waiting for her under the pillared portico of the church flooded her with warmth and strength. He wrapped his arms around her trembling shoulders. Their eyes met in love and resolve. They turned and walked into the church together, their footsteps echoing eerily in the vast hall. With Wilson and Robert's cousin as witnesses, the two lovers took their vows with little ceremony and no poetry. It was finished within minutes. Sealed to each other legally at last, they left the church by half past eleven. They separated at the church door to go to their respective homes while they waited to spirit themselves to Italy one week later. After which, they would never be separated again.

Elizabeth later wrote of her wedding day:

> *"In the emotion and confusion there was yet room in me for one thought which was not a feeling – for I thought that, of the many, many women who had stood where I stood, not one of them all, perhaps, has had reasons strong as mine for an absolute trust and devotion towards the man she married – not one!"*

Walking back into her own house at 50 Wimpole Street was agony. She had to take off her wedding ring and act as though nothing had happened. Every time the Marylebone Church bells rang she could hardly breathe. She was terrified of being found out. She felt burning guilt about leaving her sisters and brothers behind in the wake of her father's rage. She thought of the social embarrassment they would all endure. She set about writing the difficult letters of explanation. She started with the easiest – to her sisters in whose sympathies she had full confidence. Next, she wrote to her brothers, of whom she was not so sure. Finally, she wrote to intimate friends, like Mrs. Mitford and her cousin, John Kenyon. When she could put it off no longer, she wrote the dreaded letter to her father. She carefully timed the posting of the letters to arrive the day after she left.

Robert's experience was altogether different. He was elated. The headaches that he had been suffering with were gone. He was filled with energy, and he plunged into the securing of coach, train and boat tickets for their escape to the European continent. He urged Elizabeth to pack as light as possible. *"One struggle more,"* he promised, and they would be safe.

Elizabeth and Wilson packed just three small boxes and walked away from their lives and families forever. Wilson managed their trip to the railway station by cab under Robert's name. All of Robert's letters to her were in one of the boxes. She could not bear to leave them behind. Underneath her dress was a secret packet that not a soul knew about—not even Robert. It contained the forty-three sonnets that she had written over the course of their courtship. They recounted the entire story of her love for him—from the first seed of affection to the full flowering of love and passion for which she now sacrificed everything.

On Saturday, September nineteenth, at three-thirty in the afternoon, Elizabeth left the house on Wimpole Street for the last time. She carried Flush beneath one arm and had Wilson steadying her on the other. They met Robert at Hodgson's Bookshop on the corner of Marylebone and High Street. Elizabeth was in a near stupor by the time they got into the cab that Robert had hired. She later said that the whole day passed as if it were a dream.

The entire operation rested heavily on Robert's shoulders. He worried incessantly about the stress, both emotionally and physically, that the journey would have on Elizabeth's health. She had never been exposed to the noise or crowds of a railway station, let alone a rough night crossing of the English Channel.

By the time they arrived in Rouen, en route to Paris, they were all *"exhausted either by sea or sorrow."* Robert carried Elizabeth to their room through a crowd of curious onlookers.

When they arrived in Paris, they felt safe at last, far enough away from England to rest from their hectic flight. They were alive and well and in the city of light and love. There would be no more partings, no more anguished farewells, no more letters of unfulfilled longings, no more counting the hours until they were together again. How would these two dreamy poets fare together in a world unsheltered by family protection and the notion of love felt from afar? Elizabeth wrote to her sister Arabel:

> *"I am seeing near in him all that I seemed to see afar...thinking with one thought, feeling with one heart."*

After Paris, they took a lovely, long meandering route through France on their way to Italy. Travel was slow and painstaking. They covered twenty-five miles a day, yet they loved every minute of it. They gloried in being free, being together and seeing places they had only dreamed of seeing.

When they arrived in Orleans, their dream was pierced by the reality of what they had left behind. A packet of letters from her family was waiting for Elizabeth when they arrived. She asked Robert to leave the room so that she could *"meet the agony"* alone.

Her sisters' letters were just as she had hoped they would be—full of elation for her escape to liberty and happiness, as were the letters from Mrs. Mitford and John Kenyon. As for her father's letter, just seeing his handwriting on the envelope made her feel feverish. It contained what she knew it would. She was disinherited and banished from his affection forever. But it was her brothers' letters that caused her unexpected pain. They were as unforgiving as their father. They claimed she had shamed them all and was without honor. She was cast forever from their affections as well.

This was the last step in her long ordeal to be free. Her sisters and friends had not failed her. She was rejected by her father and brothers, but she now had Robert. His love eclipsed all others. She was her own woman now, making her own choices. She tucked the letters away and turned again to Robert. She chose happiness.

When they arrived in Italy, they spent their first winter in Pisa. Robert found an apartment for them close to the leaning tower. As soon as they were settled, he insisted on a period of complete rest for Elizabeth. He wanted no demands whatsoever placed upon her. He waited on her hand and foot. He even fretted if she walked across the apartment in bare feet for fear she would catch a cold. Elizabeth exulted to her sisters in her letters of having the most perfect husband in the whole world. Wilson agreed that she had never seen a man so attentive to a woman.

Elizabeth raved in her letters to her sisters about the air in Italy. She called it *"miraculous"* and was completely convinced it was healthier for her. Even when it was cold, she said that it did not have the *"metallic"* feel of England's air.

When they finally settled down to daily life in Pisa, they were jolted by this reality — none of them could cook — not even their maid, Wilson. None of them had ever lived independently before. Therefore, they had all their meals sent up from a nearby trattoria. They never knew what was being prepared for them. Elizabeth loved the daily surprise. They loved the abundant fresh fruit and vegetables in Italy. It was a welcome change from the beef and mutton of England.

After supper, Elizabeth would take a nap while Robert took a walk in the city. In the evenings, he roasted chestnuts in the fire and peeled grapes for her, and they ended their days as they had begun, laughing, talking and wrapped in each other's love. Elizabeth felt healthy, whole and loved. She wrote:

> *"Love has turned the dial backward and the joyousness of girlhood has come to me again."*

In Pisa, Elizabeth discovered that she was pregnant for the first time. It was completely unexpected, as she had assumed that she was too frail to conceive. It took her some time to acknowledge it. Wilson begged her to reduce her use of laudanum, but to no avail. Robert was nearly hysterical for fear that she would not survive the ordeal. He could not bear the thought that she could die because of his passion. She miscarried the baby at five months. When it was over, he released his anxiety for her safety and survival by throwing himself onto the bed beside her *"in a passion of tears and sobbing like a child."* Elizabeth, on the other hand, was not in the least bit depressed. She regarded her pregnancy as proof of how healthy she was getting and how thoroughly Robert had transformed her life, body and spirit as well.

After wintering in Pisa, the Browning's settled in Florence where they leased an apartment, Casa Guidi, near the Piazza San Felice. It was an odd apartment in an odd location. The building was a former palace, and the rooms were cavernous with impossibly high ceilings; yet, it was crammed into a narrow side street with no views of their beautiful city.

But there was something about it that Elizabeth loved. She said:

> "I can live here my own way and work my own work and enjoy my own silence."

The Browning's lived here for thirteen years.

It did not take Elizabeth long to adopt the identity of the country that she and Robert had chosen as a refuge. Elizabeth was having an intense love affair with Italy. She also became emotionally involved in Italian politics. Italy was occupied by Austria at the time. She identified with Italy's oppression by a foreign aggressor just as she had felt under her father's domination. She witnessed fighting in the streets of Florence from the windows of her own home. She could not fight like a soldier, but she could write like a warrior. She argued passionately for Italy's liberation from Austrian occupation in her first political poem, "Casa Guidi's Windows:"

> *"And I a singer also, from my youth... Prefer to sing with those who are awake... The further I walk into life the louder grows the battle, the quicker beats the drum in my heart."*

Robert, however, always felt like an Englishman in a strange land. His longing for his native country is immortalized by his words, *"Oh to be in England! Now that April's there..."* His chosen country was now the heart of Elizabeth. Theirs was the union of two souls which is what love should be but rarely is. Elizabeth called Robert, *"The partner of my soul."* They were so joined in mind that they felt that talking together was simply their way of thinking aloud.

Their poetry bespeaks the profound love that united two poets as husband and wife, partners for life. Robert expressed his passion for Elizabeth with unforgettable images in his poem:

Summum Bonum

*All the breath and the bloom of the year in
the bag of one bee:
All the wonder and wealth of the mine in
the heart of one gem;
In the core of one pearl all the shade and the
shine of the sea:
Breath and bloom, shade and shine, –
Wonder, wealth, and –
how far above them –
Truth, that's brighter than gem,
Trust, that purer than pearl,
Brightest truth, purest trust in the universe –
All were for me
In the kiss of one girl.*

However ideal their relationship was, it was not without its challenges. They still missed their friends and family back in England. She knew what to expect from her father, but she was struck and confused by her brothers' condemnation of her. She longed for her family to visit her in her own home in Italy and to meet her husband. She was hurt when they did not come. But she was more concerned for Robert's social needs which were much greater than her own. He was naturally energetic and social; whereas, she was *"the luxurious chair lover"* as he called her, content with her books and writing and accustomed to solitude.

They had been married for eighteen months when Elizabeth suffered a second miscarriage. The possibility of being a mother had found a home in Elizabeth's psyche, and the loss of this pregnancy was harder on her than the first. She worried that her dependence on laudanum, which Robert had begged her to give up, had contributed to the loss of the baby. Robert and her doctor also believed that her profuse letter writing had exhausted her and precipitated the miscarriage.

When she became pregnant a third time, she followed all of Robert's advice. She rested in bed most of the time. She reduced both her laudanum and her letter writing. She even engaged in that detested female pastime—sewing. She stitched a layette for the baby she was determined to keep.

Her efforts were rewarded when she gave birth to their only child on March 9, 1849, at age forty-three. Elizabeth was ecstatic that her son was not a frail, sickly child, but a *"rosy and round"* boy. The woman who had determined that she would be a poet instead of a wife and mother never ceased to marvel and give thanks that now she was all three: wife – mother – poet, just four years after meeting Robert.

Robert felt a mix of emotions as he held his new little son. To honor his mother, he and Elizabeth gave the baby her maiden name, Wiedemann—in full, Robert Wiedemann Browning. It was a distinguished name, but he was never known by it. Elizabeth nicknamed him "Penini" which meant *"little one"* in Italian. She thought it was a wonderful name because it was *"declinable"* – Penini... Peni... Pen. Pen was the name that stuck throughout his life.

The doctor would not allow Elizabeth to nurse; so Pen had a wet nurse until he was seventeen months old. She dressed her blond, curly haired, miracle baby in silks and satins, right down to his little shoes. The only member of the household that was not overjoyed by Pen's arrival was Flush. He raged. He sulked. He fell into a depression for weeks. Finally, he accepted the inevitable, and he too *"patronized the cradle."*

Three days after the baby's birth, Robert received a letter from his sister, Sarianna, telling him that his mother had died. Because Elizabeth had insisted on marrying and running away secretly, he had not been able to say goodbye to her and had not seen her since. He was devastated. Robert's depression over the death of his mother worsened throughout the spring. The only thing that brought him solace was cradling his little son. He lost his appetite, he could not sleep well, and his appearance showed it. Now, Elizabeth worried about Robert's health.

It was summertime in Florence and the heat was as oppressive as Robert's mood. Elizabeth decided that they needed a change of scenery. She arranged for the family to spend the summer in the mountain village of Bagni di Lucca, in a little house surrounded by forest *"sung to continually by a rushing mountain stream."* She was right; his outlook improved from the day they arrived.

Elizabeth encouraged Robert to walk everyday in the woods, feeling that exercising and reconnecting with nature would do him good. She often joined him, and they were both astonished by the strength and stamina she had when accompanying him on his long hikes. If Robert judged a stretch of trail to be too hard for her, he swept her up in his arms and carried her.

On one of their long afternoons in the woods, Elizabeth chose to reveal the sonnets that she had written to him during their courtship. She had kept them a secret because of early misplaced prejudices. Elizabeth had always determined to prove that she could write as academically as any man and avoided syrupy *"female"* poetry, and Robert had once made a passing remark to her against *"putting one's love into verse."* However, when Elizabeth met Robert, she released the tide of her love onto paper. She discovered the essence of poetry-- love. But Robert's profound bereavement at the loss of his mother impressed her to expose to him the record of her deepest heart, even at the risk of sounding overly sentimental.

Beneath the protection of the pines, with the soft mountain breezes whispering in collusion, she confessed...

"Do you know I once wrote some sonnets about you?"

Then, with a shy smile that would be unusual for a wife to give a husband of three years, she added nonchalantly...

"There they are, if you care to see them."

And there they were indeed — a poetical diary that documented the whole of their courtship — from her newly awakened love, to her fears and doubts, to the joy and exhilaration of their shared devotion. It was forty-four pages of the greatest love poetry ever written.

Elizabeth wrote her sister with an unusual undertone that Robert was *"much touched and pleased."* However, Robert wrote to his sister during that summer that he had come to know his wife as he had never known her before. He had been mistaken in thinking that there was nothing left to know. Their lives had come full circle. Just as Robert's love had healed and brought Elizabeth back to life, so now Elizabeth's love healed and brought Robert back to life.

The penultimate verse, Sonnet Forty-Three, is one of the most well-known and often quoted love poems of all time:

How do I love thee? Let me count the ways.
I love thee to the depth and breadth and height
My soul can reach, when feeling out of sight
For the ends of Being and ideal Grace.
I love thee to the level of everyday's
Most quiet need, by sun and candle-light.
I love thee freely, as men strive for Right;
I love thee purely, as they turn from Praise.
I love thee with the passion put to use
In my old griefs, and with my childhood's faith.
I love thee with a love I seemed to lose
With my lost saints, - I love thee with the breath,
Smiles, tears, of all my life! – and, if God choose,
I shall but love thee better after death.

Far from feeling the sonnets to be sentimental, Robert saw them for what they were — the finest sequence of sonnets in the English language since Shakespeare. Despite their intimate nature, he felt they must be published. So they disguised them as translations of foreign sonnets by giving them a misleading title, "Sonnets from the Portuguese." What the reader would not know is that *"my little Portuguese"* was a pet name Robert had given Elizabeth because of her dark complexion.

When the air of the Italian mountains began to nip their cheeks rather than caress them, Robert and Elizabeth returned to Florence vowing to establish a regular writing routine. Elizabeth had been concerned that Robert's writing in the past three years had trailed off significantly. His worries about her health and about money seemed to sap his will to write. Robert, however, was not at all troubled about it. He simply said that he would write when he was in the mood to do so. But after his emotional season of becoming a father and losing his mother, he had much to release on paper. Elizabeth, on the other hand, had always been a disciplined writer and always would be. Writing was central to her well being. She dove right in to the second installment of her political poem, "Casa Guidi's Windows."

She did not have the distractions that most mothers of toddlers have because of Wilson's devoted service to her and little Pen. She was absolutely enamored with her baby. She doted on him to the extreme. Pen was totally unscheduled and unruly. Wilson and Robert both felt that she spoiled him. But Elizabeth brushed aside their concerns. Her letters to her sisters, once full of Flush's antics, were now full of the baby's antics.

She was a progressive thinker for her time in that she believed that children were "*neuter.*" She did not think that little boys should be treated any differently than little girls. She continued to dress Pen in flouncy satins and laces well into boyhood, and she refused to cut his hair. This was fine, as long as Pen was a baby. But when he grew from baby to little boy, it became a point of contention between Robert and Elizabeth. As Pen's hair grew longer and longer, she even painstakingly curled it into the same spaniel ringlets that she wore. People on the street would admire their lovely little girl. Robert did not like it.

Robert and Elizabeth also differed as to what would be their son's primary language. Elizabeth wanted Pen to speak Italian. But Robert maintained that his son was an Englishman and he wanted him to speak the language of his heritage. They each got their way, and Pen was brought up speaking both languages. When he was little, he spoke his own unique mix of English and Italian that Elizabeth found delightful.

Now that she was a mother, Elizabeth was even more anxious to be reunited with her family and show them her wonderful child. But a trip to England was out of the question as she was pregnant again. Her fertility astonished her. She had now had four pregnancies in three years. She was as careful to keep this baby as she was with her last pregnancy. But by Christmas, she had miscarried again.

Letters from England brought happy news. Her sister, Henrietta, had finally married her long time love, Surtees Cook. Elizabeth received the news with a mix of joy and relief. She had felt so much guilt about leaving her dear siblings behind in the aftermath of their father's fury. However, it appeared that Elizabeth's courage to be true to herself had paved the way for them to do the same. Emboldened by Elizabeth's happiness with Robert, Henrietta found the courage to choose for herself when she asked Papa's permission to marry, but was refused. The brothers supported her decision but did not attend the wedding so as not to further agitate their father. To see another sister cast out of their father's affections after acting as honorably as she could, the hearts of the Barrett boys began to soften. They reopened the lines of communication with Elizabeth, deeming five years of silence punishment enough.

By the summer of 1850, Elizabeth suffered her fifth and final miscarriage. This was the most difficult one yet. She bled profusely. In an effort to stem the bleeding, her doctor packed her in ice for three days. Robert sat at her side, stroking her hands, caressing her brow and constantly encouraging her to hold on. She wrote later that she had too much to live for, Robert and her Penini, to let go.

Miraculously, Elizabeth recovered her full strength again. For one who had been plagued by weakness and ill health all her life, Elizabeth noted that she had a peculiar gift for recovering from pregnancy and miscarriages. Nevertheless, Robert continued to be even more cognizant than she about her health. For five years she had lived in a gentle climate, exercised regularly, improved her diet and reduced her dependence on opium. Yet, her happiness was the greatest benefit for her well being. Robert was ever aware that if any of these factors slipped, her health could easily decline and he was very protective of her.

The following year, they both felt that she was strong enough to travel. So the Browning's took the trip back home that they had talked about and longed for ever since they had left England. But the prospect of a homecoming came with both dread and anticipation. Robert was returning to a home without his beloved mother. Elizabeth was returning to a home with a father who would not acknowledge her existence. England was *"dear,"* but it was also *"a place of bitterness."* Their time in England had every element that they had anticipated.

It went much better for Robert than he had expected. The joy of reuniting with his father and sister soothed the pain of coming home to a motherless house more than he imagined it would. He soon found himself fully in his element again. He relished being back in London's literary circles. He had missed his friends more than he had realized and he loved introducing his wife to them. Elizabeth, in turn, loved being brought into her husband's world which included many local critics and celebrities, including the great Scottish essayist, satirist and historian, Thomas Carlyle. The former recluse was surprised at how much she enjoyed this sociability. It was yet another miraculous transformation that Robert's influence had upon her.

However, there was much to oppress Elizabeth's homecoming — starting with the air. Her old cough returned the moment she stepped on England's shore. It worsened in London. They had arranged to stay in a house just around the corner from 50 Wimpole Street. Living in her own neighborhood, continually ignored by her father and being unwelcome in her old home tormented her. She was propelled back into all her former fears and guilt even though she knew she had made the right choice.

Both she and Robert wrote Papa with appeals for forgiveness and reconciliation. He answered their petitions with a *"violent and unsparing"* letter and a packet of all the letters she had written him over the last five years — unopened. She knew her father was proud. But she had not known that he was vindictive and unyielding. A thought crept into her mind that had never been there before. Had he ever loved her? It certainly did not resemble the love she felt for her child. She later wrote to Henrietta:

> *"I could never tell you, if I tried, what I felt when those letters came back to me... all with their unbroken seals testifying to the sealed up heart which refused to be opened by me. Oh, if my child were cast out of society for the most hideous of possible crimes, could I keep my heart so sealed up towards* **him***? Not while a pulse of life stirred in it. If God and man cried*

aloud to me not to open, I should yet open — I could not help it."

Her pain was tempered by her reconciliation with her brothers and the undiluted joy of reunion with her two sisters. She met Henrietta's husband, Surtees, and their new baby boy. The three sisters talked endlessly every day, at once delving into all things profound and superficial, in a feminine communion that Robert could not penetrate. He remarked on *"the natural bond between sisters – mystifying."*

Robert could have stayed in England forever, but he could see the strain on Elizabeth's health — physically and emotionally. So at the end of September, he packed his household, which included Flush and Wilson, and returned to the continent. Robert's spirits sagged while Elizabeth's rose as they rolled out of London. From the moment she stepped onto France's shore, she pronounced the air to be *"light and clear"* and took a deep, easy breath.

The Browning's only went as far as Paris and wintered there. Over the next ten years, they lived as nomads, changing residence every three to six months. They followed the seasons and the weather, always seeking a milder climate to ease the strain on Elizabeth's lungs. They wintered in Paris, Rome as well as Florence, which they considered home, and summered in England or the Italian mountains.

After five years of astonishingly good health, Elizabeth began to experience a decline. The old heaviness in her chest returned along with chronic coughing, breathlessness, and attacks of fever, particularly during the winters. No matter where she was, cold air was always hard on her lungs.

The winter of 1851–52 was more cold and bitter than usual, bringing with it a major shift in Robert and Elizabeth's lifestyle. Aware of Robert's social nature, Elizabeth had always encouraged him to go out, whether or not she felt well enough to accompany him. She did not want her limitations to limit him. He had always resisted the suggestion, saying he only cared for her company. That worked as long as they were in Florence, which was still a sleepy little town with very little entertainment. But this winter was different. They were in Paris, the cultural center of Europe. Elizabeth desperately wanted to enjoy it, but her fragile health would not allow it. Robert, however, could breathe as well in cold as in warmth. There was no need for him to be imprisoned in a winter apartment, as was she. She could enjoy Parisian society through Robert. She had long ago learned to live vicariously through others and that old ability returned. So Robert began to make his first forays into society without her. When he returned from his outings, he would entertain her with lively stories of all that was happening in Paris. She told her sisters that she made him tell her every last detail.

This new development in their lives was another manifestation of the depth and maturity of their relationship. They each allowed the other to live at their natural pace without feeling threatened, abandoned or resentful. There was no possessive expectation that one should be the sole fulfillment of the other's happiness. They were of one heart, but not entangled. They were together yet separate — separate yet together.

The Browning's returned to England in July 1852, for a very social summer. They again took an apartment near 50 Wimpole Street where they entertained a stream of celebrity callers—the Carlyles; English philosopher, writer and painter John Ruskin; poet, politician Richard Monckton Milnes who was accompanied by Florence Nightingale, who was not yet famous.

They still could not get an audience with the man that Elizabeth wanted most to see—her father. She wrote him another letter, begging for reconciliation. When a return letter came, she pressed it close to her pounding heart and closed her eyes, uttering a prayer of hope for a benevolent content. What she found on the page instead were harsh words of reprimand, calling her to repentance:

> *"...written after six years with the plain intention of giving me as much pain as possible....Am I to repent that I did not sacrifice my life, and its affections, to the writer of that letter?"*

That night, having spent all her tears, she placed the letter in the flames of the evening fire and fell asleep, exhausted, in the arms that she knew would never close against her.

They fled the fog of London in October to return to Florence. It was a terrible journey that severely taxed Elizabeth's health. She could hardly get a breath between wrenching paroxysms of coughing. She felt like she was suffocating. Robert was frantic. He had never seen his wife so ill. He nursed her so tenderly that it brought Elizabeth to tears. She wrote to Arabel...

> *"...for a man to love a woman after six years as he loves me could only be possible to a man of very uncommon nature such as his..."*

When they reached Casa Guidi, Elizabeth immediately felt better. It felt good just to be home. She relaxed. Her breathing relaxed. Her health improved and Robert stopped worrying. Other than the lingering depression over her father's continual rejection, they passed what they would come to call *"the happy winter."*

After Paris and London, Florence was dull. But they would use it to their advantage. The time had come to do what they had always talked about doing, writing together. They would establish a new routine and stick to it, separate but together. They got up early, by seven o'clock each morning. This took a lot of discipline especially for Elizabeth who had made it a priority, since a teenager, to sleep late on doctor's orders. They dressed and took breakfast at nine. Wilson would take Pen out for the day, and the poets wrote until three in the afternoon, when they took their next meal.

Robert wrote at a desk in the little sitting room. Elizabeth wrote in the drawing room in her favorite chair with her feet up. The doors between them stayed closed. They never shared or discussed their work. Elizabeth had always been secretive about a project once she started on it. She said:

> *"An artist must, I fancy, either find or make a solitude to work in, if it is to be good work at all."*

Robert was working on a collection of lyrics called "Men and Women." Elizabeth was working on her poetical novel "Aurora Leigh." She had been mulling the project in her head for years and considered it to be her most important work. It fulfilled the supreme purpose of poetry in her opinion, which was to bring to light the moral issues of the day. The central theme of "Aurora Leigh" was the issue closest to her heart — the emancipation of downtrodden women in a male centered society.

That winter Elizabeth acquired an interest that would become an issue between her and Robert — spiritualism. Spiritualism was the vogue in Victorian times and fed into Elizabeth's spiritual nature. Robert, however, was more than skeptical; he was disgusted with the entire affair. He saw all this table moving, spirit writing and séances as so much trickery. He felt that his wife was being duped by charlatans. But her ardor for the spirits would not be quelled. They disagreed more about this than anything else.

Robert and Elizabeth, however, had a remarkable capacity to argue without anger or rift. Each respected the other's right to disagree. Their conflicts were typical of married couples — money and parenting. They openly differed on subjects that have broken countless families and friendships — politics and religion. They realized that intellectual differences were absurdly unimportant compared to love, respect, understanding and commitment.

The Browning's never left Italy that year. When summer came, they went back to the mountain resort, Bagni di Lucca. They abandoned their strict writing schedule, but they kept working in a more relaxed way. Elizabeth kept pencil and paper in her apron pockets to scribble her thoughts as they came to her — a habit also

God's Singers

shared by our two Emilys—Brontë in Yorkshire and Dickinson across the sea.

Robert worked but was easily distracted. Even Pen worked a little. Elizabeth resisted formal education for children believing that *"play is the occupation of a child – a child learns most when he plays."* This summer Pen had shown an interest in reading so she began to teach him simple words. But his attention span was short and he was slow to learn. The lessons were not very fulfilling for either of them. This engendered more exchanges between Elizabeth and Robert about Pen's general lack of discipline. Elizabeth could not understand why anyone would want to discipline this angel child. Robert was tired of Pen's lack of restraint.

As the summer waned, Robert talked of wintering in Rome. They had not been there yet, and he had heard that Rome society was equal to that of Paris. It was also rumored that certain notables would be in Rome that season—such as Charles Dickens and William Makepeace Thackeray. Elizabeth was hesitant at first, but finally agreed to go for the milder Roman climate. She was still struggling with flagging energy and a persistent cough.

Arriving there in late November, they resumed their winter habit of Elizabeth remaining at home while Robert sampled the city's delights—always bringing back plenty of stories and entertainment for her. Roman society was vibrant indeed and the climate was friendly, as promised.

At home, Elizabeth did not lack for company. Thackeray visited the Browning's quite often with his teenage daughters, Anny and Minny. Elizabeth also found a fascinating new friend in the American sculptress Harriet Hosmer. "Hatty" was twenty-two years old and lived totally independently. She lived alone and worked hard at her art everyday and dined in the cafés *"precisely as a young man would."* She did all this without losing her femininity in the process. She was a *"perfectly emancipated female."*

Rome's greatest drawback was that it was expensive. By the time spring arrived, their pocketbook was drained. They returned to Casa Guidi for the next eighteen months. They recommenced their writing routine of *"the happy winter"* and added time for Pen's education to their schedule. Pen's lack of focus and disinterest in any kind of learning finally began to concern Elizabeth. Neither she nor Robert could understand it, as they had both been child prodigies with insatiable appetites for learning. Elizabeth wrote, *"Pen is not in the least studious."* She kept his education informal, which she felt suited him. She continued with reading lessons while Robert sat at the piano with him to teach him to play. Pen displayed a strong interest in music. Elizabeth had to admit that Robert's more disciplined approach with Pen was making a difference.

Pen was nearly six years old, and Elizabeth regarded his approaching birthday with dread. She had accepted that she would have no more children, and she wanted to keep Pen a baby as long as possible. She delighted in the fact that he still talked baby talk, and she persisted in dressing him in silks and satin slippers rather than trousers and shoes. Even when he asked for his curls to be cut because they were getting in his way, she would not allow it. She had decided that age twelve was the magical age when children lost their androgyny. She seemed determined for Pen to grow at the rate she wanted, rather than the rate that came naturally to him. It was a strange reenactment of her father's parenting style—attempting to keep her child in perpetual childhood for her own comfort.

She was happy and she wanted to slow the passage of time. She felt an underlying panic that Pen was growing up. At the same time, she felt her strength fading. But one can only resist so long before time demands its due.

Her dear old friend and companion, Flush, died. He was fourteen years old. Later that winter, her longtime friend and correspondent, Mrs. Mitford died. It was a hard winter physically as well. Her chronic bronchitis returned with a vengeance. She had never been so sick in Italy. Wilson and Robert nursed her night and day, keeping the fires stoked and spoon feeding her sips of coffee to revive her. But Elizabeth was not ready to die. She had a child and a husband to live for, and she had not yet finished her masterwork, "Aurora Leigh." Her will to live persisted, and she rallied as she always did in the spring. She wrote, "*I am on my perch again – nay, even out of the cage door.*" She remarked to Harriet Hosmer, who came for Easter, that she was like a cat that had nine lives.

The Browning's had been in Italy for two years, and it was time for a trip back to England. *Aurora Leigh* was not yet finished, but Robert's collection of "Men and Women" was ready for publication. They would need to go to London to proof and publish it. Elizabeth felt that this was Robert's finest work. She was anxious for the world to acknowledge him as the poet of genius that she knew he was.

Copying, proofing and printing, all done by hand, was time consuming work. It took three months to finish the project. Elizabeth hardly had time to spend with her sisters. But Pen spent much time at 50 Wimpole Street, entertaining and being entertained by his five uncles while Mama and Papa worked. An incident occurred in the old house one day that thrilled Elizabeth *"to the roots of my heart."*

One afternoon, Pen and his Uncle George were playing boisterously in the hall during the hours that Papa Barrett was usually away. He surprised them both by walking out of the dining room to see about the noise. According to George, he watched them play for two or three minutes. Without saying a word, he returned to the dining room and called for George. He asked, *"Whose child is that, George?"* George replied, *"Ba's child."* The old man showed no emotion whatsoever. He simply followed with, *"And what is he doing here, pray?"* George's answer is not recorded. But Elizabeth had been granted, indirectly, her fondest wish. Her father had seen her child.

They returned to Paris in the fall where they received news that Robert's book was in the bookstores. Their joy was cut short when they learned that only enough copies were sold to cover printing costs. Robert was first enraged and then depressed by the reviewers who criticized him for his old fault—obscurity. Elizabeth suffered with him. Bearing the criticisms with him, they drew even closer.

Robert had had enough writing for awhile. His father, an accomplished artist, and sister, Sarianna, were now permanently residing in Paris. They were in the habit of going to the Louvre everyday with pencil and pad in hand to draw. Robert joined them. Spending his days absorbed in drawing with his loved ones was a fine remedy for his darkened mood.

Elizabeth did not argue or push him to write. She was glad he had found something to lift his spirit. The winter was upon her now, and she had six months of being shut in to finish writing *Aurora Leigh*. She turned her attention full time to what she felt was the most important thing she had ever written.

Her protagonist, Aurora Leigh, was born in Italy to an Italian mother and an English father. Her mother died at her birth, and her father died when she was thirteen. She was sent to England to be brought up by a crusty old aunt whose main concern was to marry her off to her cousin Romney, who looked forward to having a wife to help him realize his idealistic social ambitions. But Aurora had a different view of marriage as well as a strong desire to fulfill her vocation as a poet.

It came down to one central theme that is as relevant today as it was then — can women be happy with only their art to fulfill them or do they need men? She had much to draw on from her own life as she worked out her story. Though she wanted to prove Aurora independent of needing a man for fulfillment, she could not. It was not Elizabeth's truth. She had led what she believed was a complete life through her creative work alone before she met Robert; yet, her love for him had expanded and fulfilled her life beyond imagining. How could she postulate anything otherwise? Aurora Leigh found the same. She needed the love of Romney as well as her work to be completely fulfilled. Both were essential.

The Browning's spent the following summer of 1856 in England, working and visiting their friends and family. First they visited her cousin, John Kenyon, at his home on the Isle of Wight. Kenyon held a special place in their hearts, as he had been instrumental in introducing them. He was also the first to support their elopement. He not only defended them socially, but he had sent them money every month to help them get by. Now he was dying of cancer, and their visit was heavy with sad farewells.

They went from there to Somerset to visit Henrietta for the first time in her own home. It was a welcome delight after their sad stay on the Isle of Wight. Elizabeth enjoyed playing auntie to Henrietta's three children, and Pen was happier than ever running with his cousins. Elizabeth was particularly overjoyed to find that Henrietta and Surtees were just as well matched and in love as she and Robert. She called their home *"a nest of love."*

Back in London, Elizabeth supervised the publication of *Aurora Leigh*. Summer was on the wane, and she worked herself to near collapse rushing through the proofs as fast as she could before it was time to return to Italy. She never even tried to contact her father this time; all hope for reconciliation was gone.

They were back at Casa Guidi when *Aurora Leigh* came out to mixed reviews. But it was no matter. The public loved it. The first edition sold out in one week. The second printing sold out in a month. They could not be printed fast enough. Robert was more ecstatic about Elizabeth's achievement than she was. Any latent disappointment that he had from his literary failure the year before was now transformed into absolute elation over his wife's success.

A month later, in December 1856, they received news that Kenyon had died and left them a legacy in his will. With Kenyon's generosity and the proceeds from the sale of *Aurora Leigh*, they felt financially secure for the first time.

It should have been another happy winter for the Browning's at Casa Guidi, but Elizabeth could not quiet her cough, despite taking all the usual precautions. She remained sequestered in her warm, draught-free room for months. She had no energy, not even for reading or writing. With her mind unoccupied, her thoughts went to her father's indifference to her and her family. It was hard to understand and accept. She had expected a period of punishment, but it had never occurred to her that he would banish her from his affections forever.

Her malaise turned to grief when she received word from her sister, Arabel, that Papa had unexpectedly died from an acute skin infection. No one had realized he was so sick. There had been no tender last words, no forgiveness for his children who had dared to marry and there never would be. He died in the silent emotional isolation in which he lived.

His children buried him alongside his wife at Ledbury. Surtees Cook was amazed to see all the Barrett sons weeping openly at his grave. It did not appear that they had been freed from a tyrant, rather, that they had lost someone they dearly loved. Arabel's grief was short lived. She had waited out her father's domination. She was forty-three years old. She had money. She was free for the first time in her life.

Elizabeth took the news of her father's death in the same way she had taken the news of her mother's and Bro's deaths. She took to her couch for days in a state of paralytic shock. She was pale and unresponsive to Robert's entreaties of comfort. He was relieved when she finally began to cry. He was even more relieved to see that when the tears came, they were purely tears of grief, and not of self-reproach.

Her spirits were brightened by a visit from Harriet Beecher Stowe at Casa Guidi that spring. Elizabeth had long admired Harriet's work, <u>Uncle Tom's Cabin</u>, which had a theme of freedom like so much of her own work. But the two women found, to their mutual delight, that they shared another passion as well, spiritualism. They bonded immediately.

It was a relief to have the sad winter gone and to get out of her room into the sunshine. She was anxious to regain the company of her family and friends. She felt stronger, but she had lost her sense of wellness. She wrote that she felt some *"vital fluid"* had been drained from her. She attempted to replace those vital fluids with higher doses of laudanum. She was tired and did not want to travel. She wanted to stay close to home and be comfortable.

People who saw her were shocked at her decline. When American author Nathaniel Hawthorne and his wife visited that winter, he thought she looked like a dark little ghost. He described her appearance as *"elfin."* His wife wondered how such an insubstantial creature could be alive. Elizabeth described herself to Henrietta as a *"rag of a woman."*

She worked on a little bit of poetry and was amazed at the recuperative power of creative work. The poems were political verses that were decidedly anti-English and pro-Italian. She published the slim volume in March 1860. The English critics defensively condemned her, which did not bother her in the least. She took it as evidence that she had made an impact, which is exactly what she wanted to do.

Her decline continued to the point that she began to feel removed from the physical world. Robert and Pen, so full of life and vitality, seemed distant to her. She wrote:

> *"I have been very ill – nearly as ill as I could be, to come back again to the natural world… I constantly felt on the edge of a precipice."*

She had no will to eat and lived on laudanum. She was exhausted even when Robert picked her up from her bed and carried her to the drawing room to sit up in her chair.

When the news of Henrietta's death arrived, it propelled her further into her trance-like state. It was unthinkable that her dearest sister, who had always been the healthy one, had died of cancer, leaving three small children. Robert wrote to her brother George, *"The wounds of that heart never heal altogether."*

Robert took her to Rome that winter, hoping that the change of scenery and warmer weather would revive her. Their winter routine of Robert going out without her seemed desperately sad that season. To George, she wrote…

> *"I feel more fit for going to heaven sometimes... the angels there stand thicker."*

They both knew she was slipping away, but they kept up pretenses. She stayed home and read and wrote as energy would permit. Robert went out with his friends, sometimes talking and drinking into the early hours of the morning while his weakened soulmate slumbered on without resentment.

The gossiping tongues of Rome wagged that Robert was tired of his sick wife. But there were no morning recriminations between them. Their happy kisses and steady stream of talk was evidence of the enduring strength of their love. Long after the expression of their physical love became impossible, Robert could still talk to Elizabeth as if she were another part of himself. Elizabeth wrote to Sarianna:

> *"...the peculiarity of our relation is that even when he's displeased with me he thinks aloud with me and can't stop himself."*

They were both perfectly aware of how precious and extraordinary this was. Robert wrote to George that winter:

> *"Ba and I, know each other for time and I dare trust eternity. We differ...as to spirit-rapping, we quarrel sometimes about politics and estimate people's character with enormous difference, but, in the main, we **know** each other..."*

A very special memory from their last winter in Rome was a visit from Hans Christian Anderson. Elizabeth described him as, *"very earnest, very simple, very*

God's Singers

childlike." Their little winter Roman community gave a children's party for him. With the candles burning low, Hans Christian Anderson read his story, "The Ugly Duckling," to the children. After which, Robert read his children's story, "The Pied Piper of Hamlin," to the accompaniment of flute music. It was a magical evening.

In the spring they returned to Casa Guidi. Robert wanted to call in a doctor, but Elizabeth refused. She said that she was tired of doctors. There was nothing she was feeling that she had not been through before. Robert wanted to believe her, but he felt a heavy foreboding that this time was different. He sensed that she was failing. She had refused solid food for a month, living on broth and milk, and was weaker than ever.

On Friday, June 28, she seemed to brighten a bit. She let Robert sit her up in bed, as it made breathing easier for her. Wilson came in and said she was sure that Elizabeth was improving. Pen came in to say good night and asked his mother if she was feeling better. "*Much better,*" she assured him.

Robert settled himself in a chair nearby to watch through the night with her. She slept peacefully except for stirring from time to time when she would murmur his name and smile. Once she opened her eyes and told him to go to bed. There was no need to sit up with her. He checked her feet and found that they were ice cold even though the room was warm near to sweltering. At half past three, Elizabeth woke with a start. With eyes wide open and staring into space, she exclaimed, "*What a fine steamer – how comfortable.*" Robert called to their young maid, Annunciata, in alarm. Together they bathed her feet in warm water after which Robert tried to get her to take some chicken jelly.

She kissed him, clasped her arms around his neck and closed her eyes. Robert was not sure if she was asleep or awake. He whispered…

"Do you know me?"

She smiled again and murmured…

"My Robert — my heavens, my beloved!"

She kissed him again and again saying…

"Our lives are held by God."

Robert gently lowered her back onto the pillow, but she seemed unaware of the motion and continued to try to kiss him.

When she was lying down once more and could no longer reach him, she kissed her hands and reached them out to him, as if trying to cover him in kisses. He asked her…

"Are you comfortable?"

"Beautiful," she answered.

And she seemed to fall back asleep. He saw a cough rising in her chest; he lifted her up again to make it easier for her. The cough subsided and she rested her head on his chest. He looked down at her and saw her forehead wrinkle in a pang of distress. Then as quickly as it came, it cleared. In that moment, she looked like a young girl again. It was Annunciata, anxiously looking on, who realized that Elizabeth was dead and said...

"È morta."

Her tiny body, so weary from years of strain, had finally given out. Elizabeth's last gesture was to kiss Robert, her last thought was of their love. She was fifty-five years old. They had been married for fifteen years.

After her death, Robert found solace by taking pen in hand and writing to his sister, Sarianna:

> "She put her arms around me saying, 'God bless you' repeatedly — kissing me with such vehemence that when I laid her down she continued to kiss the air with her lips, and several times raised her own hands and kissed them; I said 'Are you comfortable?' 'Beautiful.' I only put in a thing or two out of the many in my heart of hearts... and she began to sleep again — the **last**, I saw. I felt she must be raised, took her in my arms, I felt the struggle to cough begin, and end unavailingly — no pain, no sigh, -- only a quiet **sight**. Her head fell on me... It was so. She is with God, who takes from me the life of my life in one sense, -- not so, in the truest. My life is fixed and sure now. I shall live out the remainder in her direct influence.
>
> "...She will be buried tomorrow... I shall now go in and sit with herself — my Ba, for ever... How she looks now — how perfectly beautiful!"

He added:

> "Pen has been perfect to me: he sat all yesterday with his arms round me; said things like her to me. I shall

try and work hard, educate him, and live worthy of my past fifteen years' happiness."

Elizabeth was buried three days later on July 1, in the Protestant Cemetery in Florence.

Robert went into a state of suspended belief. He *knew* Elizabeth was dead—he had laid her in the grave himself. But he did not *feel* she was dead. He felt her all around him, but more importantly, *in* him. He had always said that she was a part of his very soul, and she remained so now. As long as he lived, she lived.

The days passed, with his heart full of her presence. But being unable to reach out to touch her, feel her, smell her, her absence overwhelmed him. Stricken, he paced the dark echoing halls at night, crying…

"I want her. I want her."

After Elizabeth

Robert

Twenty-six days after Elizabeth was buried, Robert and Pen left Florence and boarded a train for England. Father and son were a great source of comfort and strength to each other. When his mother died, Pen seemed to grow up in a day. He was twelve years old; the age that Elizabeth had marked as the end of childhood. In keeping with her wishes and with Pen's approval, Robert cut the boys long locks off for the first time in his life. Pen finished his schooling at a formal English school.

Robert found many unpublished poems among Elizabeth's papers, some of which he felt were her best. He had them published the following year in a collection called, <u>Last Poems</u>.

He rejoined his former London literary circle, began writing again and became the literary lion that Elizabeth always knew he was. He produced an enormous amount of poetry. Half of his works were written after his wife's death. He received many honors, including an honorary degree from Oxford University. Though Elizabeth's fame had preceded his in life, his fame superseded hers after her death.

He spent his summers in France. He did not return to Italy for seventeen years. He never returned to Florence, though he must have thought about it a great deal. Perhaps he even tried to return to Florence, but in the end, could not bring himself to go.

There is a small portable tea set in a little wicker basket in the Armstrong Browning Library at Baylor University in Waco, Texas. It once belonged to Mrs. Jean Sherwood, an American literary critic. She tells an intriguing story about the tea set:

It was the summer of 1889, and she was on a train in Italy going from Venice to Florence. She was the only person in the car until an elderly man, short and stout, boarded the train and settled himself in a seat across the aisle from her. As the train moved through the countryside, he sat completely still, staring out the window, apparently lost in his own thoughts. There was no dining car on the train; so she opened her traveling tea basket and prepared some tea at her seat and took out some biscuits for an afternoon snack. As the only other person in the car was the old man, she asked him if he would like to join her. He graciously accepted her invitation and moved to sit across from her on her side of the car.

During tea, she introduced herself and explained that she was an American literary critic. He took some interest in this revelation and asked, *"Who do you think is the greatest woman poet in America?"* Mrs. Sherwood replied that America had no great women poets, but that the greatest woman poet that ever lived was Elizabeth Barrett Browning. At the sound of her name, the old man dropped back into his dreamy state, his eyes wandering from Mrs. Sherwood and their tea. In a lowered voice, he shared, *"She was my wife."* Mrs. Sherwood said that instead of taking the train on to Florence, Mr. Browning disembarked at the next stop, Bologna.

Robert never remarried and was a widower for thirty-eight years – from 1861 to 1899. He died at age eighty-seven at Pen's home, the Palazzo Rezzonico, in Venice, Italy. He never considered retiring. On the day of his death, Pen came into his father's room to tell him that his last poem, "Asolondo," had been published. Robert replied, *"How gratifying."* These were his last words.

Robert Browning is entombed at Poet's Corner at Westminster Abbey in London.

Pen

Pen may have lacked intellectual determination, but he inherited an artistic gift from his parents. After failing in school, he finally found his niche in painting and sculpting. He studied with Rodin in Paris. Though he never became a part of the British art establishment, he exhibited in both Paris and London and gained considerable respect as an artist. He created several wonderful likenesses of his father on canvas over the years. They can be seen at the Armstrong Browning Library at Baylor University in Waco, Texas.

When he was thirty-eight years old, he married American heiress, Fannie Coddington, whose father was a wealthy metal merchant. His marriage to Fannie allowed him to buy and restore the Palazzo Rezzonico on the Grand Canal in Venice. The marriage did not last, and eventually she left Pen and became a nun. They never had any children. However, Pen had an illegitimate daughter by a peasant girl with whom he had an affair while on a holiday in Brittany. This daughter, Ginevra, came to live with him during his marriage and stayed with him until she married.

After his father died and his wife left him, he sought out the old family servants, Wilson, who he called "his beloved Lily," and her husband, Ferdinando. He provided a home for them at the Palazzo Rezzonico. After Ferdinando died, Wilson moved with Pen to Asolo, Italy. Reminiscent of his mother's political activism, he invested in a lace factory to bring employment to the area.

In his later years his eyesight failed him, which hampered his painting. People remembered him as kind, portly and cheerful. He knew how to live the Italian *dolce vita*. Throughout his life, he collected writings and artifacts from his famous parents' lives, including Casa Guidi, which he hoped to make into a memorial to them. However, when he died in 1912, at age sixty-three, he had no will and everything that he possessed was sold at auction to the highest bidder.

Wilson

Wilson married the Browning's servant, Ferdinando. They had two sons. Ferdinando eventually became a cook in Venice, and they lived with Pen at the Palazzo Rezzonico. Ferdinando died in 1893. Living her last years with Pen in Asolo, her death came ten years prior to his, at age eighty-two in 1902.

As recently as the 1950's, locals in Asolo could still remember her in her old age, wandering the countryside talking to herself.

Elizabeth as a Poet

It is not surprising that the recurrent theme in Elizabeth's poetry is liberation. It underscores her own personal struggles for freedom—freedom from a domineering father, freedom from physical pain and its limitations, freedom from drug dependence, and freedom from fears and the hypochondria that kept her an invalid for years.

It is also interesting to note that her family's fortune was made through the enslavement of human beings. The Barrett's sugar plantations were worked by black slave labor, and her mother's side of the family made their fortune in the slave ships. For one whose social conscience was so keen, this must have been a shame to her. It seems as if she was trying to free herself and atone for her family history through her poetry.

Her poem, "The Cry of the Children," a poetic narrative about the horrors of child labor in the mines and factories of England, influenced child labor law in the House of Lords. She must have felt a great triumph and lifting of her spirits. It spurred her on to continued political and philosophical activism through her writing.

She wrote of the freeing of nations: Greece and Italy. The Italians were so grateful for the voice she gave to their cause in "Casa Guidi's Windows" that they placed a plaque above the door of Casa Guidi. It proclaimed that the verse of Elizabeth Barrett Browning was "*A Golden Ring*" which wedded Italy and England.

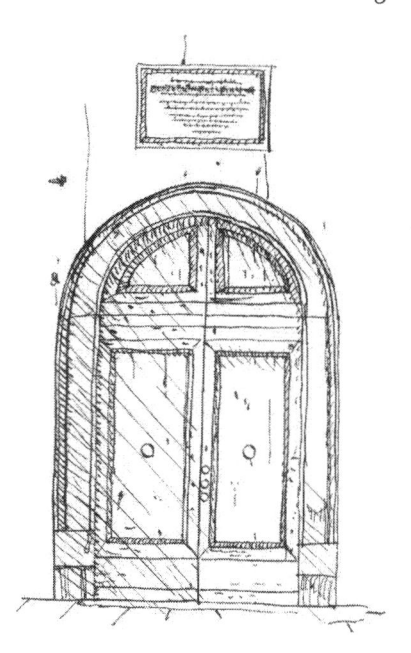

She wrote of the freeing of slaves in Greece, Russia, America and the West Indies. She wrote of freedom for women in <u>Aurora Leigh</u>, a novel in verse. In this work that is both personal and political, she questioned whether women could be happy with only their art to fulfill them or did they need marriage. Her most famous work continues to be her love poems to Robert in "Sonnets from the Portuguese."

She was considered by her contemporaries to be one of England's leading poets. She was considered for Poet Laureate of England, but Alfred Lord Tennyson was appointed instead. (After Tennyson's death, Christina Rossetti was considered for Poet Laureate.)

As a young poet, she longed for a female mentor, a literary "grandmother," but could not find one. No woman had published poetry before her. Hence, she became the literary grandmother for countless women who followed after her! She did not know, during her lifetime, about the unknown recluse in Amherst, Massachussetts, who was so inspired by her work that she kept a picture of her in her room. That poet's name was Emily Dickinson, whose work would change the face of poetry forever.

Though sentimental, Elizabeth Barrett Browning's poems possess interest, discrimination and compassion. They reveal a soul of divine understanding and expression tempered with unblushing humanity:

> *I knock and cry, - Undone, undone!*
> *Is there no help, no comfort, - none?*
> *No gleaning in the wide wheat-plains*
> *Where others drive their loaded wains?*
> *My vacant days go on, go on.*
>
> *Only to lift the turf unmown*
> *From off the earth where it has grown.*
> *Some cubit-space, and say, 'Behold,*
> *Creep in, poor Heart, beneath that fold,*
> *Forgetting how the days go on.'*
>
> *Take from my head the thorn-wreath brown!*
> *No mortal grief deserves that crown.*
> *O supreme Love, chief misery,*
> *The sharp regalia are for THEE*
> *Whose days eternally go on!*
>
> *And having in thy life-depth thrown*
> *Being and suffering (which are one),*
> *As a child drops his pebble small*
> *Down some deep well, and hears it fall*
> *Smiling – so I. THY DAYS GO ON.*

Elizabeth Barrett Browning

Life and Love

I

FAST this Life of mine was dying,
Blind already and calm as death,
Snowflakes on her bosom lying
Scarcely heaving with her breath.

II

Love came by, and having known her
In a dream of fabled lands,
Gently stooped, and laid upon her
Mystic chrism of holy hands;

III

Drew his smile across her folded
Eyelids, as the swallow dips;
Breathed as finely as the cold did
Through the locking of her lips.

IV

So, when Life looked upward, being
Warmed and breathed on from above,
What sight could she have for seeing,
Evermore . . . . but only Love?

Inclusions

OH, wilt thou have my hand, Dear, to lie along in thine?
As a little stone in a running stream, it seems to lie And pine!
Now the drop the poor pale hand, Dear, unfit to plight with thine.

II

Oh, wilt thou have my cheek, Dear, drawn closer to thine own?
My cheek is white, my cheek is worn, by many a tear run down.
Now leave a little space, Dear, lest it should wet thine own.

III

Oh, must thou have my soul, Dear, commingled with thy soul? –
Red grows the cheek, and warm the hand, the part is in the whole!
Nor hands nor cheeks keep separate, when soul is joined to soul.

Sonnet VIII

First time he kissed me, he but only kissed
The finger of this hand wherewith I write;
And ever since, it grew more clean and white,
Slow to world-greetings, quick with its "Oh, list,"
When the angels speak. A ring of amethyst
I could not wear here, plainer to my sight,
Than that first kiss. The second passed in height
The first, and sought the forehead, and half missed,
Half falling on the hair. O beyond meed!
That was the chrism of love, which love's own crown,
With sanctifying sweetness, did precede.
The third upon my lips was folded down
In perfect, purple state; since when, indeed,
I have been proud and said, "My love, my own."

Sonnet XIV

If thou must love me, let it be for naught
Except for love's sake only. Do not say,
'I love her for her smile - her look - her way
Of speaking gently,- for a trick of thought
That falls in well with mine, and certes brought
A sense of pleasant ease on such a day' -
For these things in themselves, Beloved, may
Be changed, or change for thee - and love, so wrought,
May be unwrought so. Neither love me for
Thine own dear pity's wiping my cheeks dry:
A creature might forget to weep, who bore
Thy comfort long, and lose thy love thereby!
But love me for love's sake, that evermore
Thou mayst love on, through love's eternity.

The little cares that fretted me,
I lost them yesterday
Among the fields above the sea,
Among the winds at play;
Among the lowing of the herds,
The rustling of the trees,
Among the singing of the birds,
The humming of the bees.

The foolish fears of what may happen
I cast them all away
Among the clover-scented grass,
Among the new-mown hay;
Among the husking of the corn
Where drowsy poppies nod,
Where ill thoughts die and good are born,
Out in the fields with God.

Post Script

The Armstrong Browning Library at Baylor University in Waco, Texas, is a research library devoted to the study of the lives of Robert and Elizabeth Barrett Browning. It houses the world's largest collection of books, manuscripts, letters and memorabilia pertaining to the Browning's.

Dr. A. J. Armstrong, an English professor at Baylor University, became interested in Robert Browning in the early 1900's and began to collect books and articles associated with him. In 1909, he went to Italy and met Pen Browning who was then sixty years old. He spent three days there as Pen's guest. He came away with a personal mission to pursue and acquire everything by or concerning the Browning's.

When all of Pen's belongings were auctioned off in 1913, Armstrong had an agent in London keep a record of the buyers. This enabled him to track down as many Browning items as possible and obtain them by either begging or purchasing them. Without this record and the determination of American Browning lovers, above all Dr. Armstrong and his wife, also an English professor, the Browning items would have been irretrievably scattered. Browning scholarship would have been forever diminished.

In 1918, Dr. Armstrong donated his precious acquisitions to Baylor University, founding the Armstrong Browning Library, where the work of studying the Browning's and collecting any new memorabilia continues to this day.

One of the unique aspects of the beautiful Armstrong Browning Library is its collection of sixty stained glass windows, room after room of brilliant windows depicting the poetry of both Robert and Elizabeth in a stunning medium and color. Forty of the windows represent themes from Robert Browning's poems while twelve represent Elizabeth's "Sonnets from the Portuguese." Most of the windows were commissioned in the late 1940's and early 1950's, as the edifice was being planned and built. However, the three oldest in the collection date to 1924. The newest windows are brilliant, colorful scenes of Italy. These are believed to be the largest collection of secular glass in the world.

It was through her research at the Armstrong Browning Library that Margaret Forster wrote her masterful book, _Elizabeth Barrett Browning, A Biography_, Doubleday, 1989. This was the first biography of Elizabeth written in thirty years. She also wrote _Lady's Maid_, a novel about Elizabeth Barrett Browning's personal maid, Wilson.

Postlude

William Morris, writer, artisan, and friend of Dante Gabriel Rossetti and the Pre-Raphaelites, summed up the crucial necessity of the arts to civilization when he wrote:

> *"History has remembered the kings and warriors, because they destroyed; Art has remembered the people, because they created."*

Christian Wiman, modern poet and editor of "Poetry" magazine, reprises this axiom:

> *"Let us remember that in the end we go to poetry for one reason, so that we might more fully inhabit our lives and the world in which we live them, and that if we more fully inhabit these things, we might be less apt to destroy both."*

This book is written in honor of and with gratitude for the artists of the ages who have strained to straddle heaven and earth to birth beauty from despair, to pull life from ashes, to light the darkness. They have miraculously kept us connected to both our humanity and our divinity. Without their words, their songs, their images in paint and sculpture, how could we remember who we are?

Authors' Notes

Nothing makes a subject come alive more than visiting the place where it happened. There is a lingering energy that enlarges your mind and experience when you go to the places where great minds lived and worked out the great events of their times. You no longer stand outside of history but in it. It becomes a part of you. Fortunately, historical sites connected to our poets are abundant. Retracing their paths has brought us much joy and fun over the years.

Another aspect we enjoy is to be among like-minded people who are also making a pilgrimage to these venerated sites. Gravesites, in particular, carry a feeling of hallowedness. It is not uncommon to find handwritten quotes and notes of gratitude left at an author's headstone. Admirers leave a multitude of meaningful gifts—pencils, pens, pebbles, pinecones, flowers. Our favorite ritual is to place a penny for the poets' thoughts at their gravesites. It is small payment, indeed, for the wealth of words and wisdom that they left behind.

We highly recommend visiting these places if you can.

Emily Dickinson—Massachusetts
Amherst—The Homestead and The Evergreens
West Cemetery on Triangle Street—Emily's gravesite
Amherst College—Frost Library Special Collections

Christina Rossetti—England
London—Highgate Cemetery—Christina's gravesite

Emily Brontë — Yorkshire, England
Haworth — The Parsonage, St. Michael's Church, The Black Bull Inn
Dewsbury — Site of Miss Wooler's Roe Head School
Scarborough — Anne's gravesite

Elizabeth Barrett Browning — England, Italy, Texas
London, England:
Wimpole Street — Barrett family home, Regent's Park
Marylebone Church — Site of Elizabeth and Robert's secret marriage
Westminster Abbey — Robert's grave at Poets' Corner
British Library — original manuscripts
Italy:
Florence — Casa Guidi — Browning home
Protestant Cemetery — Elizabeth's gravesite
Venice — Palazzo Rezzonico — Pen's home and Robert's death site
Waco, Texas:
Armstrong Browning Library — Largest collection of Browning artifacts in the world

About the Authors

Lisa Mayo Murphy was born in San Jose, California but considers herself an All-American girl, having lived in eight states in all four quadrants of the country. Her love for European History and Literature took root when she lived and studied in Paris, France, before receiving her Bachelor's degree in French language from Brigham Young University. She has pursued her lifelong passion for the arts by extensive reading, writing, teaching and travel. She is married to Shaun Murphy. They have three children who are the joy of their lives.

Leanne Mayo was born and grew up in California. She attended San Jose State University and graduated from Brigham Young University. She has taught in both public and private schools. She is married to Raymond Mayo. They are the parents of six children, and they have seven grandsons and seven granddaughters. She has had a lifelong love for and appreciation of the fine arts. She has studied art history and was a docent at the Utah Museum of Fine Arts at the University of Utah for ten years. Most recently, she and Raymond lived and traveled in China and set up an English language program for a software company there. Leanne has spoken to literary, school and women's groups from British Columbia to Florida. She shares the biographies and works of famous literary figures, including the poets in this book. Currently, she lives in Midway, Utah, with her husband of over fifty years. She is also the author of <u>Shakespeare in a Nutshell</u>.

Bibliography

Emily Dickinson

Bolin, Frances Schoonmaker,
Poetry for Young People — Emily Dickinson, Sterling Publishing Company, Inc., New York, 1994.

Brownell, Johanna (edited by),
Emily Dickinson Poems, Castle Books, Edison, New Jersey, 2000.

Farr, Judith,
The Passion of Emily Dickinson, Harvard University Press, Cambridge, Massachusetts, London, England, 1992.

Habegger, Alfred,
My Wars Are Laid Away In Books, Random House, New York, 2001.

Hart, Ellen Louise. Smith, Martha Nell, (edited by).
Open Me Carefully — Emily Dickinson's Intimate Letters to Susan Huntington Dickinson, Paris Press, Ashfield, Massachusetts, 1998.

Johnson, Thomas H. (edited by),
The Complete Poems of Emily Dickinson, Little Brown and Company, Boston. New York. Toronto. London, 1960.

Longsworth, Polly,
<u>The World of Emily Dickinson, A Visual Biography</u>,
W.W. Norton & Company, New York. London, 1990.

Moore, Christopher (introduction by),
<u>Emily Dickinson Selected Poems</u>, Gramercy Books, New York. Avenel. New Jersey, 1993.

Moore, Geoffrey, (edited by),
<u>Great American Poets Emily Dickinson</u>, Clarkson N. Potter, Inc., New York, 1986.

Showalter, Elaine,
<u>A Jury of Her Peers</u>, Vintage Books, A Division of Random House, Inc., New York, 2009.

Whicher, George Frisbie,
<u>This Was a Poet, A Critical Biography of Emily Dickinson</u>, Amherst College Press, Massachusetts, 1992.

Emily Brontë

Barker, Juliet,
<u>The Brontës: A Life in Letters</u>, The Overlook Press, Woodstock & New York, 2002.

Birrell, Augustine,
<u>Life of Charlotte Brontë</u>, Walter Scott, LTD., London,____.

Davies, Stevie,
<u>Emily Brontë: Heretic</u>, The Women's Press Ltd, 34 Great Sutton Street, London E CIV, 1994.

Emily Brontë, Poet of Solitude, http://www.hermitary.com/solitude/Brontë.html, 2008.

Emily Brontë Selected Poems, Bloomsbury Poetry Classics, St. Martin's Press, New York, 1994.

Evans, Barbara and Gareth Lloyd,
Everyman's Companion to the Brontës, J. M. Dent & Sons Ltd., London and Melbourne, 1982.

Frank, Katherine,
A Chainless Soul – A Life of Emily Brontë, Fawcett Columbine, New York, 1990.

Fraser, Rebecca,
The Brontës – Charlotte Brontë and Her Family, Crown Publishers, Inc., New York, 1988.

Gérin, Winifred,
Emily Brontë, A Biography, Oxford University Press, Walton Street, Oxford OX2 6DP, 1978.

Gordon, Lyndall,
Charlotte Brontë – A Passionate Life, W. W. Norton & Company, New York, London, 1994.

Howard, Tom,
Brontë Country, Regency Publishing House, Ltd., London, 1995.

Peters, Margot,
Unquiet Soul, Atheneum, New York, 1986.

Vicary, Tim,
The Brontë Story, Oxford University Press, 1991.

Christina Rossetti

Battiscombe, Georgina,
Christina Rossetti: A Divided Life, New York, Holt, Rinehart and Winston, 1981.

Crump, R. W. (text by),
Christina Rossetti, The Complete Poems, Penguin Books Ltd., 80 Strand, London WC2R ORL, England, 1990.

Gaetano Polidori,
http://en.wikipedia.org/wiki/Gaetano_Polidori, 2010.

Golden Head by Golden Head, by Dante Gabriel Rossetti,http://victorianweb.org/art/illustration/dgr/2.html, 1862.

Hubbard, Elbert,
Little Journeys, Volume 2, The World Publishing Company, Cleveland, Ohio, New York, New York, The Roycrofters, 1928.

Jones, Kathleen,
Learning Not To Be First – The Life of Christina Rossetti, St. Martin's Press, New York, 1991.

Negri, Paul (edited by),
English Victorian Poetry An Anthology, Dover Publications, Inc., Mineola, New York, 1999.

Porter, Peter (edited by),
Great English Poets Christina Rossetti, Clarkson N. Potter Inc., New York, 1986.

Project Canterbury, Christina Georgina Rossetti, London: Catholic Literature Association, http://anglicanhistory.org/bios/cgrossetti.html, 1933.

Rossetti, W.M. (ed.),
Christina Rossetti – Poetical Works, 1904, http://www.canamus.org/Enchiridion/Xtrs/rsetiwmr.htm

Sawtell, Margaret,
Christina Rossetti – Her Life and Religion, A. R. Mowbray & Co., Limited, London, 1955.

The Germ. Thoughts toward Nature in Poetry, Literature, and Art, William Michael Rossetti, Biography, http://www.rossettiarchive.org/docs/ap4.g415.raw. html, 2010.

Thomas, Frances,
Christina Rossetti, The Self Publishing Association Ltd, Units 7/10 Hanley Workshops, Hanley Road, Hanley Swans, Worcs., England, 1992.

Elizabeth Barrett Browning

Cooks, John D. Stevenson, Lionel,
English Literature of the Victorian Period, Appleton – Century – Crofts, Inc., New York, 1949.

Forster, Margaret,
Elizabeth Barrett Browning – A Biography, Doubleday, New York, 1989.

Forster, Margaret,
<u>Lady's Maid</u>, Fawcett Columbine, New York, 1990.

Hubbard, Elbert,
<u>Little Journeys, Volume 2</u>, The World Publishing Company, Cleveland, Ohio, New York, New York, The Roycrofters, 1928.

Macy, John,
<u>The Story of the World's Literature</u>, Garden City Publishing Company, New York, 1925.

Porter, Peter (edited by),
<u>Great English Poets — Elizabeth Barrett Browning</u>, Clarkson N. Potter, Inc., New York, 1992.

Ricks, Christopher,
<u>The Brownings – Letters and Poetry</u>, International Collectors, Garden City, New York, 1970.

Simons, Judy,
<u>Diaries and Journals of Literary Women from Fanny Burney to Virginia Woolf</u>, University of Iowa Press, Iowa City, 1990.

Stern, Robert,
<u>Love Affairs That Have Made History</u>, The New Home Library, New York, 1942.

Untermeyer, Louis (selected by),
<u>Love Poems of Elizabeth Barrett Browning and Robert Browning</u>, Barnes & Noble Books, New York, 1994.

Winwar, Frances,
<u>The Immortal Lovers, Elizabeth Barrett and Robert Browning</u>, Harper & Row, New York, Evanston, London, 1950.

Printed in Great Britain
by Amazon